Out of the Dark

Essays, Lectures, and Addresses on Physical and Social Vision

By Helen Keller

Published by Pantianos Classics

ISBN-13: 978-1-78987-574-4

First published in 1912

Helen Keller, 1912

Contents

Preface

This volume contains all hitherto uncollected magazine articles and addresses which seem for any reason worth preserving in book form. The second article, "How I became a Socialist," was printed in the New York *Call*. Briefly it sums up my position at the present time. Of the articles on blindness, some were written in behalf of work which has since been successfully started. They are, therefore, somewhat out of date. But I have left them unchanged because they record the conditions of the blind at the time they were written, and by no means all the things advocated have been attempted in all parts of the country. There are still States in which the plea of ten years ago is pertinent to-day.

The symbol, sign, and instrument
Of each soul's purpose, passion, strife,
Of fires in which are poured and spent
Their all of love, their all of life.
feeble, mighty human hand!
fragile, dauntless human heart!
The universe holds nothing planned
With such sublime, transcendent art!"

— Helen Fiske Jackson

The *American Magazine,* December, 1912.

The Hand of the World

As I write this, I am sitting in a pleasant house, in a sunny, wide-windowed study filled with plants and flowers. Here I sit, warmly clad, secure against want, sure that what my welfare requires the world will give. Through these generous surroundings I feel the touch of a hand, invisible but potent, all-sustaining — the hand that wove my garments, the hand that stretched the roof over my head, the hand which printed the pages that I read.

What is that hand which shelters me? In vain the winds buffet my house and hurl the biting cold against my windows: that hand still keeps me warm. What is it that I may lean upon it at every step I take in the dark, and it fails me not? I give wondering praise to the beneficent hand that ministers to my joy and comfort, that toils for the daily bread of all. I would gratefully acknowledge my debt to its capability and kindness. I pray that some hearts may heed my words about the hand of the world, that they may believe in the coming of that commonwealth in which the gyves shall be struck from the wrist of Labour, and the pulse of Production shall be strong with joy.

All our earthly well-being hangs upon the living hand of the world. Society is founded upon it. Its lifebeats throb in our institutions. Every industry, every process is wrought by a hand, or by a superhand — a machine whose mighty arm and cunning fingers the human hand invents and wields. The hand embodies its skill, projects, and multiplies itself in wondrous tools, and with them it spins and weaves, ploughs and reaps, converts clay into walls, and roofs our habitations with trees of the forest. It compels Titans of steel to heave incredible burdens, and commands the service of nimble lackeys which neither groan nor become exhausted. Communication between mind and mind, between writer and reader, is made possible by marvellous extensions of the might of the hand, by elaborate reduplications of the many-motioned fingers. I have touched one of those great printing-presses in which a river of paper flows over the types, is cut, folded, and piled with swift precision. Between my thoughts and the words which you read on this page a thousand hands have intervened; a hundred shafts of steel have rocked to and fro, to and fro, in industrious rhythm.

The hand of the world! Think how it sends forth the waters where it will, to form canals between the seas, and binds the same seas with thought incorporate in arms of stone! What is the telegraph cable but the quick hand of the world extended between the nations, now menacing, now clasped in brotherhood? What are our ships and railways but the feet of man made swift and strong by his hands? The hand captures the winds, the sun, and the lightnings, and despatches them upon errands of commerce. Before its irresistible blows mountains are beaten small as dust. Huge derricks — prehensile power magnified in digits of steel — rear factories and palaces, lay stone upon stone in our stately monuments, and raise cathedral spires.

On the hand of the world are visible the records of biology, of history, of all human existence since the day of the "first thumb that caught the trick of thought." Every hand wears a birth-seal. By the lines of the thumb each of us can be identified from infancy to age. So by the marks on the hand of the world its unmistakable personality is revealed. Through suffering and prosperity, through periods of retrograde and progress, the hand keeps its identity. Even now, when the ceaseless ply of the world-shuttles is so clamorous and confused, when the labour of the individual is lost in the complexities of production, the old human hand, the symbol of the race, may still be discerned, blurred by the speed of its movements, but master and guide of all that whirring loom.

Study the hand, and you shall find in it the true picture of man, the story of human growth, the measure of the world's greatness and weakness. Its courage, its steadfastness, its pertinacity make all the welfare of the human race. Upon the trustworthiness of strong, toil-hardened hands rests the life of each and all. Every day thousands of people enter the railway train and trust their lives to the hand that grasps the throttle of the locomotive. Such responsibility kindles the imagination! But more profound is the thought that the destiny and the daily life of mankind depend upon countless obscure hands that are never lifted up in any dramatic gesture to remind the world of their existence. In "Sartor Resartus" Carlyle expresses our obligation to the uncelebrated hands of the worker:

"Venerable to me is the hard Hand; crooked and coarse; wherein notwithstanding lies a cunning virtue, indefeasibly royal, as of the Sceptre of this Planet... Hardly entreated Brother! For us was thy back so bent, for us were thy straight limbs and fingers so deformed: thou wert our Conscript, on whom the lot fell, and fighting our battles wert so marred. For in thee, too, lay a god-created Form, but it was not to be unfolded; encrusted must it stand with the thick adhesions and defacements of Labour: and thy body, like thy soul, was not to know freedom."

But wherefore these deformities and defacements? Wherefore this bondage that cramps the soul? A million tool-hands are at our service, tireless and efficient, having neither heart nor nerve. Why do they not lift the burden from those bowed shoulders? Can it be that man is captive to his own machine, manacled to his own handiwork, like the convict chained to the prison-wall that he himself has built? Instruments multiply, they incorporate more and more of the intelligence of men; they not only perform coarse drudgery, but also imitate accurately many of the hand's most difficult dexterities. Still the God-created Form is bowed. Innumerable souls are still denied their freedom. Still the fighter of our battles is maimed and defrauded.

Once I rejoiced when I heard of a new invention for the comfort of man. Taught by religion and a gentle home life, nourished with good books, I could not but believe that all men had access to the benefits of inventive genius. When I heard that locomotives had doubled in size and speed, I thought: "The food of the wheat-fields will come cheaper to the poor of the cities now," and I was glad. But flour costs more to-day than when I read of those great new engines. Why do not improved methods of milling and transportation improve the dinner of the poor? I supposed that in our civilization all advances benefited every man. I imagined that every worthy endeavour brought a sure reward. I had felt in my life the touch only of hands that uphold the weak, hands that are all eye and ear, charged with helpful intelligence. I believed that people made their own conditions, and that, if the conditions were not always of the best, they were at least tolerable, just as my infirmity was tolerable.

As the years went by and I read more widely, I learned that the miseries and failures of the poor are not always due to their own faults, that multitudes of men, for some strange reason, fail to share in the much-talked-of progress of the world. I shall never forget the pain and amazement which I felt when I came to examine the statistics of blindness, its causes, and its connection with other calamities that befall thousands of my fellow-men. I learned how workmen are stricken by the machine hands that they are operating. It became clear to me that the labour-saving machine does not save the labourer. It saves expense and makes profits for the owner of the machine. The worker has no share in the increased production due to improved methods; and, what is worse, as the eagle was killed by the arrow winged with his own feather, so the hand of the world is wounded by its own skill. The multipotent machine displaces the very hand that created it. The productivity of the machine seems to be valued above the human hand; for the machine is often left without proper safeguards, and so hurts the very life it was intended to serve.

Step by step my investigation of blindness led me into the industrial world. And what a world it is! How different from the world of my beliefs! I must face unflinchingly a world of facts — a world of misery and degradation, of blindness, crookedness, and sin, a world struggling against the elements, against the unknown, against itself. How reconcile this world of fact with the bright world of my imagining? My darkness had been filled with the light of intelligence, and, behold, the outer day-lit world was stumbling and groping in social blindness! At first I was most unhappy; but deeper study restored my confidence. By learning the sufferings and burdens of men, I became aware as never before of the life-power that has survived the forces of darkness, the power which, though never completely victorious, is continuously conquering. The very fact that we are still here carrying on the contest against the hosts of annihilation proves that on the whole the battle has gone for humanity. The world's great heart has proved equal to the prodigious undertaking which God set it. Rebuffed, but always persevering; self-reproached, but ever regaining faith; undaunted, tenacious, the heart of man labours toward immeasurably distant goals. Discouraged not by difficulties without, or the anguish of ages within, the heart listens to a secret voice that whispers: "Be not dismayed; in the future lies the Promised Land."

When I think of all the wonders that the hand of man has wrought, I rejoice, and am lifted up. It seems the image and agent of the Hand that upholds us all. We are its creatures, its triumphs, remade by it in the ages since the birth of the race. Nothing on earth is so thrilling, so terrifying, as the power of our own hands to keep us or mar us. All that man does is the hand alive, the hand manifest, creating and destroying, itself the instrument of order and demolition. It moves a stone, and the universe undergoes a readjustment. It breaks a clod, and new beauty bursts forth in fruits and flowers, and the sea of fertility flows over the desert.

With our hands we raise each other to the heights of knowledge and achievement, and with the same hands we plunge each other into the pit. I have stood beside a gun which they told me could in a few minutes destroy a town and all the people in it. When I learned how much the gun cost, I thought: "Enough labour is wasted on that gun to build a town full of clean streets and wholesome dwellings!" Misguided hands that destroy their own handiwork and deface the image of God! Wonderful hands that wound and can bind up, that make sore and can heal, suffering all injuries, yet triumphant in measureless enterprise! What on earth is like unto the hands in their possibilities of good and evil? So much creative power has God deputed to us that we can fashion human beings round about with strong sinews and noble limbs, or we can shrivel them up, grind living hearts and living hands in the mills of penury. This power gives me confidence. But because it is often misdirected, my confidence is mingled with discontent.

"Why is it," I asked, and turned to the literature of our day for an answer, "why is it that so many workers live in unspeakable misery?" With their hands they have builded great cities and they cannot be sure of a roof over their heads. With their hands they have opened mines and dragged forth with the strength of their bodies the buried sunshine of dead forests, and they are cold. They have gone down into the bowels of the earth for diamonds and gold, and they haggle for a loaf of bread. With their hands they erect temple and palace, and their habitation is a crowded room in a tenement. They plough and sow and fill our hands with flowers while their own hands are full of husks.

In our mills, factories, and mines, human hands are herded together to dig, to spin, and to feed the machines that they have made, and the product of the machine is not theirs. Day after day naked hands, without safeguard, without respite, must guide the machines under dangerous and unclean conditions. Day after day they must keep firm hold of the little that they grasp of life, until they are hardened, brutalized. Still the portent of idle hands grows apace, and the hand-to-hand grapple waxes more fierce. O pitiful blindness! O folly that men should allow such contradictions — contradictions that violate not only the higher justice but the plainest common sense. How do the hands that have achieved the *Mauretania* become so impotent that they cannot save themselves from drowning? How do our hands that have stretched railways and telegraphs round the world become so shortened that they cannot redeem themselves?

Why is it that willing hands are denied the prerogative of Labour, that the hand of man is against man? At the bidding of a single hand thousands rush to produce, or hang idle. Amazing that hands which produce nothing should be exalted and jewelled with authority! In yonder town the textile mills are idle, and the people want shoes. Fifty miles away, in another town, the shoe factories are silent, and the people want clothes. Between these two arrested forces of production is that record of profits and losses called the *Market*. The buyers of clothes and shoes in the market are the workers themselves; but they cannot buy what their hands have made. Is it not unjust that the hands of the world are not subject to the will of the workers, but are driven by the blind force of Necessity to obey the will of the few? And who are these few? They are themselves the slaves of the Market and the victims of Necessity.

Driven by the very maladjustments that wound it, and enabled by its proved capacity for readjustment and harmony, society must move onward to a state in which every hand shall work and reap the fruits of its own endeavour, no less, no more. This is the third world which I have discovered. From a world of dreams I was plunged into a world of fact, and thence I have emerged into a society which is still a dream, but rooted in the actual. The commonwealth of the future is growing surely out of the state in which we now live. There will be strife, but no aimless, self-defeating strife. There will be competition, but no soul-destroying, hand-crippling competition. There will be only honest emulation in cooperative effort. There will be example to instruct, companionship to cheer, and to lighten burdens. Each hand will do its part in the provision of food, clothing, shelter, and the other great needs of man, so that if poverty comes all will bear it alike, and if prosperity shines all will rejoice in its warmth.

There have been such periods in the history of man. Human nature has proved itself capable of equal cooperation. But the early communist societies of which history tells us were primitive in their methods of production — half civilized, as we say who dare call our present modes of life civilization! The coming age will be complex, and will relinquish nothing useful in the methods which it has learned in long struggles through tyrannies and fierce rivalries of possession. To the hand of the world belongs the best, the noblest, the most stupendous task, the subjection of all the forces of nature to the mind of man, the subjection of physical strength to the might of the spirit. We are still far from this loftiest of triumphs of the hand. Its forces are still to be disciplined and organized. The limbs of the world must first be restored. In order that no limb may suffer, and that none may keep the others in bondage, the will of the many must become self-conscious and intelligently united. Then the hand — the living power of man, the hewer of the world — will be laid with undisputed sway upon the machine with which it has so long been confounded. There will be abundance for all, and no hands will cry out any more against the arm of the mighty. The hand of the world will then have achieved what it now obscurely symbolizes — the uplifting and regeneration of the race, all that is highest, all that is creative, in man.

How I Became a Socialist

A letter printed in the New York *Call*, November 3, 1912.

For several months my name and Socialism have appeared often together in the newspapers. A friend tells me that I have shared the front pages with baseball, Mr. Roosevelt, and the New York police scandal. The association does not make me altogether happy, but, on the whole, I am glad that many people are interested in me and in the educational achievements of my teacher, Mrs. Macy. Even notoriety may be turned to beneficent uses, and I rejoice if the disposition of the newspapers to record my activities results in bringing more often into their columns the word Socialism. In the future I hope to write about Socialism, and to justify in some measure the great amount of publicity which has been accorded to me and my opinions. So far I have written little and said little about the subject. I have written a few letters, notably one to Comrade Fred Warren which was printed in the Appeal to Reason. I have talked to some reporters, one of whom, Mr. Ireland, of the New York World, made a very flattering report and gave fully and fairly what I said. I have never been in Schenectady. I have never met Mayor Lunn. I have never had a letter from him, but he has sent kind messages to me through Mr. Macy. Owing to Mrs. Macy's illness, whatever plans I had to join the workers in Schenectady have been abandoned.

On such negative and relatively insignificant matter have been written many editorials in the capitalist press and in the Socialist press. The clippings fill a drawer. I have not read a quarter of them, and I doubt if I shall ever read them all. If on such a small quantity of fact so much comment has followed, what will the newspapers do if I ever set to work in earnest to write and talk in behalf of Socialism? For the present I should like to make a statement of my position and correct some false reports and answer some criticisms which seem to me unjust.

First — How did I become a Socialist? By reading. The first book I read was Wells's "New Worlds for Old." I read it on Mrs. Macy's recommendation. She was attracted by its imaginative quality, and hoped that its electric style might stimulate and inspire me. When she gave me the book, she was not a Socialist and she is not a Socialist now. Perhaps she will be one before Mr. Macy and I have done arguing with her.

Mr. Wells led to others. I asked for more books on the subject, and Mr. Macy selected some from his library of Socialist literature. He did not urge them on me. He merely complied with my request for more. I do not find him inclined to instruct me about Socialism; indeed, I have often complained to him that he did not talk to me about it as much as I should like.

My reading has been limited and slow. I take a German bimonthly Socialist periodical printed in braille for the blind. (Our German Comrades are ahead of us in many respects.) I have also in German braille Kautsky's discussion of the Erfurt Programme. The other Socialist literature that I have read has been spelled into my hand by a friend who comes three times a week to read to me whatever I choose to have read. The periodical which I have most often requested her lively fingers to communicate to my eager ones is the *National Socialist*. She gives the titles of the articles and I tell her when to read on and when to omit. I have also had her read to me from the *International Socialist Review* articles the titles of which sounded promising. Manual spelling takes time. It is no easy and rapid thing to absorb through one's fingers a book of fifty-thousand words on economics. But it is a pleasure, and one which I shall enjoy repeatedly until I have made myself acquainted with all the classic Socialist authors.

In the light of the foregoing I wish to comment on a piece about me which was printed in the *Common Cause* and reprinted in the *Live Issue*, two anti-Socialist publications. Here is a quotation from that piece:

"For twenty-five years Miss Keller's teacher and constant companion has been Mrs. John Macy, formerly of Wrentham, Mass. Both Mr. and Mrs. Macy are enthusiastic Marxist propagandists, and it is scarcely surprising that Miss Keller, depending upon this lifelong friend for her most intimate knowledge of life, should have imbibed such opinions."

Mr. Macy may be an enthusiastic Marxist propagandist, though I am sorry to say he has not shown much enthusiasm in propagating his Marxism through my fingers. Mrs. Macy is not a Marxist, not a Socialist. Therefore, what the *Common Cause* says about her is not true. The editor must have invented that, made it out of whole cloth, and if that is the way his mind works, it is no wonder that he is opposed to Socialism. He has not sufficient sense of fact to be a Socialist or anything else intellectually worth while.

Consider another quotation from the same article. The headline reads:

"Schenectady Reds Are Advertising; Using Helen Keller, the Blind Girl, to Receive Publicity."

Then the article begins:

"It would be difficult to imagine anything more pathetic than the present exploitation of poor Helen Keller by the Socialists of Schenectady. For weeks the party's press agencies have heralded the fact that she is a Socialist, and is about to become a member of Schenectady's new Board of Public Welfare."

There is a chance for satirical comment on the phrase, "the exploitation of poor Helen Keller." But I will refrain, simply saying that I do not like the hypocritical sympathy of such a paper as the *Common Cause,* but I am glad if it knows what the word "exploitation" means.

Let us come to the facts. When Mayor Lunn heard that I might go to Schenectady he proposed to the Board of Public Welfare that a place be kept on it for me. Nothing was printed about this in the *Citizen,* Mayor Lunn's paper. Indeed, it was the intention of the board to say nothing about the matter until after I had moved to Schenectady. But the reporters of the capitalist press got wind of the plan, and one day, during Mayor Lunn's absence from Schenectady, the *Knickerbocker Press* of Albany made the announcement. It was telegraphed all over the country, and then began the real newspaper exploitation. By the Socialist press? No, by the capitalist press. The Socialist papers printed the news, and some of them wrote editorials of welcome. But the *Citizen,* Mayor Lunn's paper, preserved silence and did not mention my name during all the weeks when the reporters were telephoning and telegraphing and asking for interviews. It was the capitalist press that did the exploiting. Why? Because ordinary newspapers care anything about Socialism? No, of course not; they hate it. But because I, alas, am a subject for newspaper gossip. We got so tired of denying that I was in Schenectady that I began to dislike the reporter who first published the "news."

The Socialist papers, it is true, did make a good deal of me after the capitalist papers had "heralded the fact that I am a Socialist." But all the reporters who came to see me were from ordinary commercial newspapers. No Socialist paper, neither the *Call* nor the *National Socialist,* ever asked me for an article. The editor of the *Citizen* hinted to Mr. Macy that he would like one, but he was too fine and considerate to ask for it point-blank.

The *New York Times* did ask me for an article. The editor of the *Times* wrote assuring me that his paper was a valuable medium for reaching the public and he wanted an article from me. He also telegraphed asking me to send him an account of my plans and to outline my ideas of my duties as member of the Board of Public Welfare of Schenectady. I am glad I did not comply with his request, for some days later the *Times* made me a social outcast beyond the range of its righteous sympathies. On September 21st there appeared in the Times an editorial called "The Contemptible Red Flag." I quote two passages from it:

"The flag is free. But it is none the less detestable. It is the symbol of lawlessness and anarchy the world over, and as such is held in contempt by all right-minded persons."

The bearer of a red flag may not be molested by the police until he commits some act which the red flag justifies. He deserves, however, always to be regarded with suspicion. By carrying the symbol of lawlessness he forfeits all right to respect and sympathy."

I am no worshipper of cloth of any colour, but I love the red flag and what it symbolizes to me and other Socialists. I have a red flag hanging in my study, and if I could I should gladly march with it past the office of the *Times* and let all the reporters and photographers make the most of the spectacle. According to the inclusive condemnation of the *Times* I have forfeited all right to respect and sympathy, and I am to be regarded with suspicion. Yet the editor of the *Times* wants me to write him an article! How can he trust me to write for him if I am a suspicious character? I hope you will enjoy as much as I do the bad ethics, bad logic, bad manners that a capitalist editor falls into when he tries to condemn the movement which is aimed at his plutocratic interests. We are not even entitled to sympathy, yet some of us can write articles that will help his paper to make money! Probably our opinions have the same sort of value to him that he would find in the confession of a famous murderer. We are not nice, but we are interesting.

I like newspaper men. I have known many, and two or three editors have been among my most intimate friends. Moreover, the newspapers have been of great assistance in the work which we have been trying to do for the blind. It costs them nothing to give their aid to work for the blind and to other superficial charities. But Socialism — ah, that is a different matter! That goes to the root of all poverty and all charity. The money power behind the newspapers is against Socialism, and the editors, obedient to the hand that feeds them, will go to any length to put down Socialism and undermine the influence of Socialists.

When my letter to Comrade Fred Warren was published in the *Appeal to Reason,* a friend of mine who writes a special department for the Boston *Transcript* made an article about it and the editor in chief cut it out.

The Brooklyn *Eagle* says, apropos of me and Socialism, that Helen Keller's "mistakes spring out of the manifest limitations of her development. "Some years ago I met a gentleman who was introduced to me as Mr. McKelway, editor of the Brooklyn *Eagle*. It was after a meeting that we had in New York in behalf of the blind. At that time the compliments he paid me were so generous that I blush to remember them. But now that I have come out for Socialism he reminds me and the public that I am blind and deaf and especially liable to error. I must have shrunk in intelligence during the years since I met him. Surely it is his turn to blush. It may be that deafness and blindness incline one toward Socialism. Marx was probably stone deaf and William Morris was blind. Morris painted his pictures by the sense of touch and designed wallpaper by the sense of smell.

Oh, ridiculous Brooklyn *Eagle*! What an ungallant bird it is! Socially blind and deaf, it defends an intolerable system — a system that is the cause of much of the physical blindness and deafness which we are trying to prevent. The Eagle is willing to help us prevent misery, provided, always provided, that we do not attack the industrial tyranny which supports it, and stops its ears, and clouds its vision. The *Eagle* and I are at war. I hate the system which it represents, apologizes for, and upholds. When it fights back, let it fight fair. Let it attack my ideas and oppose the aims and arguments of Socialism. It is not fair fighting or good argument to remind me and others that I cannot see or hear. I can read. I can read all the Socialist books I have time for, in English, German, and French. If the editor of the Brooklyn *Eagle* should read some of them he might be a wiser man and make a better newspaper. If I ever contribute to the Socialist movement the book that I sometimes dream of, I know what I shall name it: "Industrial Blindness and Social Deafness. "

An Appeal to Reason

A letter published in the *Appeal to Reason* in December, 1910.

I enclose a check to be used for subscriptions to the *Appeal to Reason*. I am prompted to this by indignation at the unrighteous conviction of the editor, Mr. Fred Warren. I believe that the conviction is unrighteous, although I have arrived at this conclusion with some hesitancy. For a mere woman, denied participation in government, must needs speak timidly of the mysterious mental processes of men, and especially of ermined judges. No doubt any layman would give offence who should be guilty of the indiscretion of criticising the decisions of a high court. Still, the more I study Mr. Warren's case in the light of the Constitution of the United States, which I have under my fingers, the more I am persuaded either that I do not understand it, or that the judges do not. I used to honour our courts, which, I was told, were no respecters of persons. I was glad and proud in the thought of our noble heritage — a free law open to all children of the nation alike. But I have come not only to doubt the divine impartiality ascribed to our judiciary, but also to question whether our judges are conspicuous for simple good sense and fair dealing. We may be pardoned if we regard some of their decisions merely as human imperfection, as results of our common mortality, dependent for their seeming iniquity upon our poor human prejudice and ignorance.

Are these not the facts: Several years ago three officers of the Western Federation of Miners were indicted for a murder committed in Idaho. They were in Colorado and the governor of that State did not extradite them. They were kidnapped and brought to an Idaho prison. They applied to the Supreme

Court for a writ of habeas corpus, on the ground that they were illegally held because they had been illegally captured. The Supreme Court replied: "Even if it be true that the arrest and deportation of Pettibone, Moyer, and Haywood from Colorado was by fraud and connivance, to which the governor of Colorado was a party, this does not make out a case of violation of the rights of the appellants under the Constitution and the laws of the United States."

Some time later ex-Governor Taylor of Kentucky was indicted for murder and was wanted in his State. Mr. Warren offered a reward for the capture of Mr. Taylor and his return to the Kentucky authorities. I understand that it is not an unusual thing for a private citizen to aid in this way in the apprehension of a fugitive from justice.

To what twistings, turnings, and dark interpretation must the judges of the Circuit Court be driven in order to send Mr. Warren to prison! As I understand it, a federal law defining the kind of matter which it is a crime to mail has been stretched to cover his act. What was the act? The offer of a reward was printed on the outside of envelopes mailed at Girard by Mr. Warren. This was construed as threatening because it was an encouragement to others to kidnap a man under indictment. This the Supreme Court had by implication declared to be an innocent act. For in the case of Pettibone, Moyer, and Haywood the accomplished act of kidnapping was held to be no infringement of the rights of a citizen.

One need not be a Socialist to realize the significance, the gravity, not of Mr. Warren's offence, but of the offence of the judges against the Constitution of the United States and against democratic rights. It is provided that, "Congress shall make no law...abridging the freedom of speech or of the press." Surely this means that we are free to print and mail any innocent matter. What Mr. Warren printed and mailed had been established as innocent. What beam was in the eye of the judges of the Supreme court or what mote was in the eye of the justices of the circuit courts? It is evident that their several decisions do not stand in the same light. It has been my duty, my life work, to study physical blindness, its causes and its prevention. I learn that our physicians are making great progress in the cure and prevention of blindness. What surgery of politics, what antiseptic of common sense and right thinking, shall be applied to cure the blindness of our judges and to prevent the blindness of the people who are the court of last resort?

The Worker's Right

A letter written to the strikers at Little Falls, N. Y., November, 1912.

I am sending the check which Mr. Davis paid me for the Christmas sentiments I sent him. Will you give it to the brave girls who are striving so courageously to bring about the emancipation of the workers at Little Falls?

They have my warmest sympathy. Their cause is my cause. If they are denied a living wage, I also am defrauded. While they are industrial slaves, I cannot be free. My hunger is not satisfied while they are unfed. I cannot enjoy the good things of life which come to me, if they are hindered and neglected. I want all the workers of the world to have sufficient money to provide the elements of a normal standard of living — a decent home, healthful surroundings, opportunity for education and recreation. I want them to have the same blessings that I have. I, deaf and blind, have been helped to overcome many obstacles. I want them to be helped as generously in a struggle which resembles my own in many ways.

Surely the things that the workers demand are not unreasonable. It cannot be unreasonable to ask of society a fair chance for all. It cannot be unreasonable to demand the protection of women and little children and an honest wage for all who give their time and energy to industrial occupations. When indeed shall we learn that we are all related one to the other, that we are all members of one body? Until the spirit of love for our fellowmen, regardless of race, colour or creed, shall fill the world, making real in our lives and our deeds the actuality of human brotherhood — until the great mass of the people shall be filled with the sense of responsibility for each other's welfare, social justice can never be attained.

The Modern Woman

The Metropolitan Magazine, October, November, December, 1912.

I - The Educated Woman

What I shall try to say in the following pages is in the nature of a composite reply to letters I receive from young women who ask my advice about the education they should strive for, and the use of the education they have. The prevailing spirit of these correspondents is an eager desire to be of service. Their letters are at once delightful and appalling; they fill me with mingled pride and timidity. They reveal an immeasurable will-to-serve, an incalculable soul-power waiting, like a mountain reservoir, to be released in irresistible floods of righteousness, capable, too, of devastating misdirection. All this power says to me in so many words: "Tell us what to do."

My sense of responsibility is lightened by the consideration that people do not take one's advice, even when it is good, and when they seek it. Human actions are shaped by a thousand forces stronger than the written wisdom of the wisest guide that ever lived. The best that the seers of the race discovered centuries ago has not, it seems, become a controlling motive even in the lives of their followers. If the counsel of the ages is not regarded, an ordinary modern cannot hope that his words will have much influence for good. But a sincere request demands a sincere compliance. Since my correspondents think that my advice may be of use to them, I will suggest some problems for them to study, that they may be better fitted for humanitarian work.

Because I am known to be interested in bettering the condition of the blind, many of my correspondents, whose hearts are stirred by the thought of blindness, offer to help their brothers in the dark, and they ask me how to begin. Of late I have found that my letters, in reply to those who wish to help the blind, contain a paragraph about the sightless, and then pass to other things. I have sometimes wondered if my friends were not puzzled rather than helped by what I wrote. A class of college girls in an institution near great manufacturing cities and coal-mines asked me to initiate them into philanthropic endeavour for the sightless. I told them to study the life that swarms at their very doors — the mill-hands and the miners. I wonder if they understood. I tried to tell them what has been said many times, that the best educated human being is the one who understands most about the life in which he is placed, that the blind man, however poignantly his individual suffering appeals to our hearts, is not a single, separate person whose problem can be solved by itself, but a symptom of social maladjustment.

That sounds discouragingly vague and cosmic. It may have perplexed the girls to whom I wrote it. They asked me how to help the blind, how to educate themselves so that they might be of use to their unfortunate fellowmen, and I offered them the universe — I gravely recommended that they study Industrial Economics. My advice to them to study the life that surrounds them was perhaps the only part of my prescription that was not paradoxical. For the whole situation is paradoxical and confused. Society is a unit; the parts depend on one another; one part of the world suffers because the rest is not right. And yet we can each know only a very little about the whole of society. Moreover, these college girls, living in a life that I do not know, send their questions to me across a thousand miles — to me who must grope about a library of a few hundred books, whereas they have all the books of the world open to them. They can visit and talk with ten human beings while I am spelling out my intercourse with one.

Education? How can any one who has eyes to see and ears to hear and leisure to read and study remain uneducated? Are the "educators" at fault? Is there something lacking in those who administer the schools and colleges? I wonder about these things and puzzle out the details of my message with increasing perplexity.

The unfortunate are not only those whose infirmity appeals to our sympathies by its visible, palpable terror — the blind, the deaf, the dumb, the halt, the crooked, the feebleminded, the morally diseased. The unfortunate include the vast number of those who are destitute of the means and comforts that promote right living and self-development. The way to help the blind or any other defective class is to understand, correct, remove the incapacities and inequalities of our entire civilization. We are striving to prevent blindness. Technically we know how to prevent it, as technically we know how to have clean houses, pure food, and safe railways. Socially we do not know how, socially we are still ignorant. Social ignorance is at the bottom of our miseries, and if the function of education is to correct ignorance, social education is at this hour the most important kind of education.

The educated woman, then, is she who knows the social basis of her life, and of the lives of those whom she would help, her children, her employers, her employees, the beggar at her door, and her congressman at Washington. When Shakespeare wrote "Hamlet," or whether he wrote it or not, seems relatively unimportant compared with the question whether the workingwomen in your town receive a living wage and bear their children amid proper surroundings. The history of our Civil War is incomplete, as taught in the schools, if fifty years afterward the daughters and granddaughters of veterans do not understand such a simple proposition as this: "The woman who bears a child risks her life for her country."

It is just such fundamental propositions related to the problems of life which school education seems to ignore. In school and college we spend a great deal of time over trivial matters. I cannot recall much that I learned at Radcliffe College, which now stands forth in my mind as of primary importance. The little economic theory that I learned was admirably put; but I have never succeeded in bringing it into harmony with the economic facts that I have learned since. The courses I took were so elementary that I should not presume to judge the opportunities which Radcliffe offers for the study of economics. It simply happens, as it happens in the experience of many students, that such academic wisdom as I was privileged to share in did not touch the problems I met later.

If we women are to learn the fundamental things in life, we must educate ourselves and one another. And we few who are unfairly called educated because we have been to college must learn much, and forget much, if we are not to appear as useless idlers to the millions of workingwomen in America. Any girl who goes to school can study and find out some of the things that an educated American woman ought to know. For instance, why in this land of great wealth is there great poverty? Any intelligent young woman like those who write to me, eager to help the sightless or any other unfortunate class, can learn why such important work as supplying food, clothing, and shelter is ill-rewarded, why children toil in the mills while thousands of men cannot get work, why women who do nothing have thousands of dollars a year to spend.

There is an economic cause for these things. It is for the American woman to know why millions are shut out from the full benefits of such education, art, and science as the race has thus far achieved. We women have to face questions that men alone have evidently not been quite able to solve. We must know why a woman who owns property has no voice in selecting the men who make laws that affect her property. We must know why a woman who earns wages has nothing to say about the choice of the men who make laws that govern her wages. We must know why a hundred and fifty of our sisters were killed in New York in a shirt-waist factory fire the other day, and nobody to blame. We must know why our fathers, brothers, and husbands are killed in mines and on railroads. We women, who are natural conservationists, must find out why the sons we bring forth are drawn up in line and shot. We must organize with our more enlightened brothers and declare a general strike against war. My father was a Confederate soldier, and I respect soldiers. But I grow more and more suspicious of the political powers that take men away from their work and set them shooting one another. Not all the military poems that I have read have roused in me an heroic desire to welcome my brother home with a bullet in his heart. We women have the privilege of going hungry while our men are in battle, and it is our right to be widowed and orphaned by political stupidity and economic chaos. To be sure, we are not allowed to vote for or against the congressman who declares war; but we can instruct ourselves unofficially in these matters.

Does what I mean by an educated woman become clearer? It ought to be clear; for all that I have said was said before I was born, and said by men; so there can be no flaw in the logic. We women must educate ourselves, and that without delay. We cannot wait longer for political economists to solve such vital problems as clean streets, decent houses, warm clothes, wholesome food, living wages, safeguarded mines and factories, honest public schools. These are our questions. Already women are speaking, and speaking nobly, and men are speaking with us. To be sure, some men and some women are speaking against us; but their contest is with the spirit of life. Lot's wife turned back; but she is an exception. It is proverbial that women get what they are bent on getting, and circumstances are driving them toward education.

The other day the newspapers contained an item which is pertinent here, since we are dealing with women and education. The Harvard Corporation has voted that it will not allow any halls of the university to be open to lectures and addresses by women, except when they are especially invited by the Corporation. There was no such rule until an undergraduate club asked Mrs. Pankhurst to speak. Then the rule was made. The Corporation has a right to make such a rule. But why has it discriminated against women? An educated man is one who receives, fosters, and contributes to the best thought of his time. By this definition, are the Harvard Corporation educated men? [1]

Fortunately, education does not depend on educational institutions any more than religion depends on churches. Says Bacon in "Novum Organum": "In the customs and institutions of schools, academies, and colleges, and similar bodies destined for the abode of learned men, and the cultivation of learning, everything is found adverse to the progress of science, for the lectures and exercises are there so ordered that to think or speculate on anything out of the common way can hardly occur to any man, and if one or two have the boldness to use any liberty of judgment, they must undertake the task all by themselves; they can have no advantage from the company of others. And if they can endure this also, they will find their industry and largeness of mind no slight hindrance to their fortune. For the studies of men in these places are confined and, as it were, imprisoned in the writings of certain authors, from whom, if any man dissent, he is straightway arraigned as a turbulent person, and an innovator."

Perhaps the first lesson to be learned by us women who are bent on educating ourselves is, that we are too docile under formal instruction. We accept with too little question what the learned tell us. Reason, or whatever substitute heaven has given to us, does not stand at the door of receptivity and challenge what seeks admission. I am surprised to find that many champions of woman, upholders of "advanced ideas," exalt the intelligence of the so-called cultivated woman. They portray her as an intellectual prodigy to whom the wisest man would resign his library and his laboratory with a feeling of dismayed incompetence. It is not woman's intelligence that should be insisted upon, but her needs, her responsibilities, her functions. The woman who works for a dollar a day has as much right as any other human being to say what the conditions of her work should be. It is just this, I am sorry to find, which educated women do not always understand. They argue that because George Eliot wrote great novels, and Jeanne d'Arc led armies to victory, therefore, women have as much genius as men; so they go on and on in a course of thought which is beside the point. Those who argue against the rights to which we are plainly entitled do not elude the issue with more wavering uncertainty than we show in defending ourselves.

I am not disposed to praise the educated woman, as we commonly use the term. I find her narrow and lacking in vision. Few women whom I meet take a deep interest in the important questions of the day. They are bored by any problem not immediately related to their desires and ambitions. Their conversation is trivial and erratic. They do not consider a subject long enough to find out that they know nothing about it. How seldom does the college girl who has tasted philosophy and studied history relate philosophy and the chronicles of the past to the terrific processes of life which are making history every day! Her reputed practical judgment and swift sympathy seem to become inoperative in the presence of any question that reaches to a wide horizon. Her mind works quickly so long as it follows a traditional groove. Lift her out of it, and she becomes inert and without resource. She is wanting in reflection, originality, independence. In the face of opposition to a private interest or a primitive instinct she can be courageous and vividly intelligent. But she retreats from general ideas as if they did not concern her, when in point of fact civilized life is comprehended in general ideas.

Such a woman comes to the gravest responsibilities like the foolish virgins who hastened to the marriage with no oil in their lamps. She is not prepared for the battle of life. Before she knows it she may be in the midst of the fight, undisciplined and disorganized, struggling for all that is precious to her against an enemy whose position she has not reconnoitred. She sends her sons and daughters into the streets of life without the knowledge that protects. Ignorance gives her confidence, and she is fearless from want of understanding.

It is not possible to refer a complex difficulty to a single cause. But it sometimes seems that the heaviest shackle on the wrists of delicate, well-nurtured women is a false notion of "purity and womanliness." We are taught, generation after generation, that purity and womanliness are the only weapons we need in the contest of life. With this shield and buckler we are assured of all possible safety in an essentially hard world. But the enemy does not play fair. He disregards womanliness and purity. Women have learned this in lifelong suffering. Yet some of those who have suffered most cling to the ideal and pass it on to their daughters, as slaves teach their children to kiss their chains. About matters that affect our very lives we are cautioned to speak "with bated breath," lest we offend the proprieties and provoke a blushing disapprobation. The ideal of the trustful, pure, and ignorant woman is flattering and sweet to her timid soul. But it is not, I believe, the product of her own imagination. It has grown up in the worshipful fancy of romantic man — her poet and her master. The time has come when woman is subjecting this ideal to shrewd criticism.

[1] Since the above was written the Harvard Corporation's ruled that no one, man or woman, shall use the college lecture halls for "persistent propaganda" about social, economic, political or religious questions. In other words, the Harvard Corporation is sole judge of what a lecturer shall talk about.

II - My Lady

All things uncomely and broken, all
   things worn out and old,
The cry of a child by the roadway,
   the creak of a lumbering cart,

The heavy steps of the ploughman
   splashing the wintry mould,
Are wronging your image that blossoms
   a rose in the deeps of my heart.

The wrong of unshapely things is a wrong
   too great to be told;
I hunger to build them anew, and sit on a
   green knoll apart.

With the earth and the sky and the water
   re-made, like a casket of gold,
For my dreams of your image that blossoms
   a rose in the deeps of my heart.

These beautiful verses by Mr. Yeats are the song of the new spirit hymning the mistress of the world. The old chivalry couched a lance against dragons that would devour us, and sang our beauty in unmeasured ecstasy. In some legends it proved its gallantry by kissing an ugly hag, and forthwith she turned into a lovely princess. When we were locked in grim dungeons, chivalry assailed the stronghold and delivered us, especially if we were handsome and of royal blood.

The new chivalry is dressed in working clothes, and the dragons it must face are poverty, squalor, industrial slavery. The distressed damsel in the moonlit tower has become the girl in the street, the woman prisoned in a dirty kitchen, the wage-earner in the factory. Our champion need not fare forth into far countries to do wonders and attest his prowess. The enemy is here, everywhere — "all things uncomely and broken."

Woman-worship, the central motive of song and legend these many centuries, has been too much inspired by the will to possess and too little by the will to serve. The modern knight *sans peur et sans reproche* must learn that virtues ascribed to his lady to make her a more precious object of desire have not proved good working substitutes for some plainer virtues which he denies her after he has won his suit. It is but niggardly largess to bestow upon her so much education as will make her a witty, pleasant companion and then refuse her access to the wider knowledge of which man is the jealous custodian. We confess our incapacities. We *are* inconsistent and timid. We hand down from mother to daughter ideals of ourselves which are not in keeping with our experience. We amuse our brothers by irreconcilable and conflicting assertions. Every day of our lives we justify that superior masculine smile which says, "Just like a woman!" We especially justify it by accepting the legendary ideal of us which he has made for his gratification. This ideal has tender and beautiful aspects. But it is full of contradictions and absurdities. It is, on the whole, an obstacle to justice, intervening darkly between the facts of life and a clear, honest vision.

Men assure us that woman is an angel, but has not sense enough to share in the management of common earthly affairs. The standard of good sense which man has in mind is not an absolute standard beyond the reach of human attainment, but the ordinary standard of masculine achievement. Man ascribes to woman a mysterious short-cut method of mind known as "intuition," a cerebral power which guides all her activities from sewing on a button to discharging statesman's duties as Queen of England. Perception, tact, sympathy, nervous rapidity of thought are her age-long attributes. But — she would abuse the ballot. Her judgment is childish, she lacks discrimination and balance. She is frugal, a sharp bargainer in the retail market, a capable partner in a little shop; but she is unable to figure the economy of spending a hundred and fifty millions for battleships. She excels in organizing and conducting philanthropic work; but it would be disastrous to allow her an equal voice in determining how much public money should be spent in charitable undertakings.

I was once a member of the Massachusetts Commission for the Blind. We had forty thousand dollars of public money to spend. The work was so new and experimental that the Legislature and other officers of government could not know whether we were using the money wisely or not. There were three men on the commission and one other woman. She and I were in a safe minority, but our voice counted in every expenditure. The money was appropriated by a legislature of men as the result of an investigation and appeal made largely by women. Now note the contradiction. Women were allowed to have authority in spending State money. But no woman had had direct voice in deciding whether or not the money should be appropriated at all. The money was collected from tax-payers, many of whom were women, and it was created in part by the labour of women wage-earners. Once in the hands of the State, it was beyond the control of woman's fine, feminine intuition, of her perception, her tact, her other adorable qualities. If a woman, unaided and triumphantly irrational, should devise a situation as contradictory as that, the magnificent male would smile in condescension and say: "There you are! You see, women are utterly inconsistent."

For her to answer as she might, I fear, would be "unladylike." True ladies do not argue. They cannot argue because they are women as well as ladies, and lack the reasoning faculties. Moreover, argument is unseemly in them. It only demonstrates their proverbial loquacity. It is, in a word, "unladylike." So round and round runs the circle of thought, coming back always to that ideal of the lady; receptive, unquestioning, illogical, charming. While her lord sings to "Highland Mary," to "the angel in the house," to the "phantom of delight," it is not gentle for her to lay her hand across the sweet strings and ask a plain question. Hers is the charm "to haunt, to startle, to waylay," but she must haunt with a smile, she must startle only pleasant sensations, she must waylay her lord's thought only when it is happy, never when it is errant fallacy.

The books of the world have sung woman's praises and placed her a little higher than the angels. But the book of woman is not unmixed adoration. When desire liberates his generosity and wakes his lyre to rapture, man sets her upon peaks limitlessly high, and if she had true modesty, she would blush with discomfort at his impetuous hyperbole. However, he has his hours of disillusion and takes back everything nice he has said. As long ago as when the Hebrews were making the Bible, when man did all the writing, if not most of the talking, he discovered many faults in woman and set them down in vigorous words. He noted especially her tendency to infringe upon his hours of wordless meditation. Saith Ecclesiasticus: "As the climbing up of a sandy way is to the feet of the aged, so is a wife full of words to a quiet man."

St. Paul says: "Let the woman learn in silence with all subjection, but I suffer not a woman to teach, or to usurp authority over the man, but be in silence."

It was St. Paul who insisted on the ideal of celibacy which was taken up by the early fathers of the Roman Church. The ancient Jews had felt the need of sons to make their tribes strong against enemies; so fruitfulness with them was a religious virtue. But the Roman world was densely populated, and the need for individual salvation was more urgent than the need for more people; so single blessedness became a religious virtue among the early Christians. The natural obstacle to celibacy was woman, and the result was that she was held responsible for man's lapses into matrimony. To the more austere fathers of the church she seemed to be man's greatest enemy, his tempter and affliction, the devil's gateway, destroyer of God's image. This idea of her fitted well with the story of her misdeed in the garden of Eden and man's banishment from paradise, for which he bore her a grudge. As a wife she was not worshipped; but her unmarried state became exalted in the figure of the Virgin Mary. Men knelt to her and besought her intercession. While the spirit of the time, embodied in church authority, beautified the mother of Christ, it continued to degrade her sisters. They were shut up in convents and ordered to stay at home, to conceal their beauty as dangerous to the beholder.

The ascetic ideal did not prevail in practice because human nature is against it. The church, which found in the words of St. Paul only a reluctant approval of marriage, finally took marriage under its protection and sanctified it. The romantic spirit grew up through the Middle Ages, and woman again became an object of delight and praise. But priestcraft and statecraft, expressions of man's attitude, kept her subjugated. Man was her sole instructor in religion, and religion comprehended all that she officially learned. He taught her her duties, her needs, and her capacities. He marked out for her the wavering line which delimited her "sphere." The chief content of this "sphere" was her duty to make him happy, to be a proper mate for him. He drilled her in morals, that she might not deceive him; he taught her obedience, that she might be his slave. He celebrated her in song and story because that celebration gave him pleasure. It was an utterance of his artistic sense. He made her laws, constituted himself judge, jury, jailer, and executioner. He had entire charge of her prisons and convents, of her house, her church, and her person. He burnt her, tortured her, gave her to wild beasts and cast her forth to be a pariah when she violated his property title in her. He laid down the measure of her knowledge, the quantity of it that would meet his approval. Through all times he granted her the privilege — of bearing his children. But once born, they were his children, not hers.

One day, when he felt especially good-humoured, he gave her permission to learn to read. "I wish," said Erasmus when he was translating the Greek Testament, "that the weakest women might read the Gospels and the Epistles of St. Paul." The alphabet was her new tree of knowledge. She had made a ruinous blunder at the first tree, but the fruits of the new tree carried no penalty, except the sorrow which knowledge brings to the innocent. It is likely, however, that experience had already taught her the full measure of sorrow. The beginning of literacy among women was the beginning of their emancipation, just as the spread of common school education was the beginning of democracy. The emancipation is not complete, and we have not arrived at democracy. The masters seem instinctively to have felt that some bars should be left up, some gates should be closed against women and against certain classes of men. The professions were placarded, "Dangerous. Women not admitted." Over the pulpit was placed the legend inherited from the Jewish and Roman priesthood, "Woman, be silent."

As late as the nineteenth century John Ruskin, who was thought very radical in his time, confessed how quaintly old-fashioned he was in these words: "There is one dangerous science for women — one which let them beware how they profanely touch — that of theology." As if the relation between God and man were a masculine monopoly! Ruskin's essay on "Queens' Gardens" is an expression of the romantic liberal who dares and retreats, sings brave paeans of deliverance and then shrinks back into a sort of timid severity. He attributes to us almost every admirable quality that a human being could dream of possessing. Indeed, he praises us unfairly at the expense of our brothers; for he says: "Men are feeble in sympathy and contracted in hope; it is you only who can feel the depths of pain and conceive the way of its healing." That is to say, our natures are richer than men's, we suffer more, yet we must not explore the relations between God and man by which our sufferings are explained and assuaged. It is amusing to remember that critics have spoken of Ruskin's genius as "feminine."

The nineteenth century with its tardy medievalism and its return to lights that never were on land or sea, together with its scientific clarity and its economic revolts, has summed up all the confusions of woman's position. Ruskin and Spencer are contemporaries. Mill's "On the Subjection of Women" and Tennyson's "Princess" are fruits of the same nation and the same era.

There is a deeper comedy in the "Princess" than Tennyson intended to put there. The opening scene is on an English lawn, and there is light talk about culture and the nobility of legendary women. One of the guests mocks at the notion of women's colleges:

> Pretty were the sight
> If our old halls could change their sex, and flaunt
> With prudes for proctors, dowagers for deans,
> And sweet girl graduates in their golden hair.
> I think they should not wear our rusty gowns,
> But move as rich as emperor-moths.

Then the poet tells a sweet, fantastic story laid in Fairyland. The mood of the story is expressed in the sad, exquisite interludes, lyrics of tears, of dead warriors, and of soft yieldings to the touch of man. Poetry is timeless; but time brings its revenges even upon poets. Just before Tennyson, who had been a brave democrat in his youth, was made a baron, Newnham College was opened, and "sweet girl graduates" became so familiar that the "Princess" lost its mild point before the author was dead. Tennyson fluttered a little way into the thought of his time, and then fluttered back again. In the second "Locksley Hall," he poetized his Toryism finally and fatally. Meanwhile the world had moved on.

In the nineteenth century Shakespeare was rediscovered and worshipped the other side idolatry. Everything was found in Shakespeare, including much that is not there; for example: his profound psychological knowledge of women. Books were written about his heroines which prove that the ideal of the perfect lady is drawn forever in the Shakespearian drama. In the introductions to the plays that I read at college, Rosalind and Portia are analyzed as if the whole philosophy of womanhood were contained in their poetical fancies, or at least as if we could never thoroughly understand women without knowing what Shakespeare wrote about them. I doubt if the women in Shakespeare's comedies are to be taken seriously. They are pretty creatures intended to be played by boys. They are the vehicle of any more or less fitting strain of poetry which happens to please the poet. Alice in Wonderland is a very real little girl; but one would not make a grave, scholarly analysis of the traits of character which she displays in her encounter with the Mock Turtle. Neither should we press too heavily upon Shakespeare's poetry to extract his beliefs about women. The unrivalled sonnets voice the praise and also the petulant dissatisfaction of a man in love, or pretending to be in love for the purpose of poetry. The woman-worship in the sonnets and in the glowing passages of the plays, spoken by gallants in pursuit of their ladies, is only the conventional romanticism common in mediaeval and renaissance literature.

Shakespeare's phrasing outflies that of all other poets. But his ideas of women are neither original nor enlightened. In studying the social ideas of a writer and his time we often learn more from his unconscious testimony than from his direct eloquence. Portia is wise, witty, learned, especially when disguised as a man; but she is disposed of without protest, through her father's will and its irrational accidents, to a commonplace, bankrupt courtier, and the tacit implication is that she is happily bestowed. Where Shakespeare brings Portia's career to an end, a modern comedy would begin. In the other plays the delightful heroine is hurried off at the close of the fifth act into the possession of a man whom she would not look at if she were as wise and strong and witty as the situations have represented her. Wedlock, no matter what the conditions, or how deep its essential indignity, is good enough for the loveliest Shakespearian maiden, and there is no suggestion that all is not as it should be. Helena, devoted, brave, loyal, is rewarded by being given to a careless worthless youth. In "Twelfth Night," Viola and the sentimental Duke, Olivia and Sebastian, pair off as nimbly as if personality were only a matter of wigs and disguises, of identities easily mistaken and as easily reestablished. Hermione, queenly and gracious, is bound to a person who behaves like a furious spoilt child, and is represented as respecting him and wishing to keep him.

Shakespeare does teach us much about the ideals of women that prevailed in his time. For he regards as a comic situation, to be turned with his magic phrases and concluded with joy-bells, what we should regard as a tragic situation.

The tragedy that lurks behind the false ideal of womanhood is being disclosed in our time. Woman is beginning to say to her master: "Romantic man, cease a while your singing of lays antique and ballads new. We would talk with you in prose. You have dreamed long enough of the lady, who, alas, is in a negligible minority. It is time for you to give your superior intelligence to the well-being of millions and millions of women."

III - The Woman and Her House

We women have often been told that the home contains all the interests and duties in which we are concerned. Our province is limited by the walls of a house, and to emerge from this honourable circumscription, to share in any broad enterprise, would be not only unladylike, but unwomanly. I could not help thinking of this the other day when I was asked to go to a far state and take part in some work that is being done for the blind. If I accepted this invitation, should I not be leaving my proper sphere, which is my home? I have thought of it many times since I learned that there are in America over six million women wage-earners. Every morning they leave their homes to tend machines, to scrub office-buildings, to sell goods in department stores. Society not only permits them to leave their proper sphere; it forces them to this unwomanly desertion of the hearth, in order that they may not starve. Oh, my sisters in the mills and shops, are you too tired, too indifferent to read the ridiculous arguments by which your rights are denied and your capacities depreciated in the sacred name of the home and its defence?

Woman's sphere is the home, and the home, too, is the sphere of man. The home embraces everything we strive for in this world. To get and maintain a decent home is the object of all our best endeavours. But where is the home? What are its boundaries? What does it contain? What must we do to secure and protect it?

In olden times the home was a private factory. The man worked in the field or at his handicraft, while the woman made food and clothes. She shared in out-of-door labour; but indoor work naturally became her special province. The household was the centre of production, and in it and about it man supplied himself with all that he needed — or all that he had — by rudimentary hand-processes. The mill to grind corn was not far away. The leather used by the shoemaker was from a beef killed by a neighbour. Over every cottage door the words might have been written: "Mr. and Mrs. Man, Manufacturers and Dealers in General Merchandise." Home life and industrial life were one.

To-day they are widely separated. Industries that used to be in the house are spread all over the world. The woman's spinning-wheel and part of her kitchen and dairy have been taken away from her. When she seeks to understand economic affairs, and to exert her authority in their management, she is in reality only following her utensils.

The spinning-wheel, ancient emblem of domestic industry, has been removed to great factories. She has followed it there both as worker and owner. So she still does her part in the great task of clothing the human race. Where the spinning-wheel is, the woman has an ancestral right to be. For no matter how complex wheel and loom have become, she depends on them still to make the blanket that covers her child in its sleep. It is her duty as a house-mother to watch her spinning-wheel, to see that no member of the world-family goes ill-clad in an age when wool is abundant, when cunning machines can make good coats, when a ragged frock on a self-respecting woman is a shame to us all. It is for woman to follow her wheel, to make sure that it is spinning wool and not grinding misery, that no little child is chained to it in a torture of day-long labour. The spinning-wheel has grown a monstrous thing. In order to identify it, one must study wages, tariffs, dividends, the organization of labour and factory sanitation. The woman who studies these problems and insists on having a voice in their solution is in her home as truly as was her grandmother whose tireless foot drove the treadle of the old spinning-wheel. The home is where those things are made without which no home can be comfortable.

Once the housewife made her own butter and baked her own bread; she even sowed, reaped, threshed, and ground the wheat. Now her churn has been removed to great cheese and butter factories. The village mill, where she used to take her corn, is to-day in Minneapolis; her sickle is in Dakota. Every morning the express company delivers her loaves to the local grocer from a bakery that employs a thousand hands. The men who inspect her winter preserves are chemists in Washington, Her ice-box is in Chicago. The men in control of her pantry are bankers in New York. The leavening of bread is somehow dependent upon the culinary science of congressmen, and the washing of milk-cans is a complicated art which legislative bodies, composed of lawyers, are trying to teach the voting population on the farms.

It would take a modern woman a lifetime to walk across her kitchen floor; and to keep it clean is an Augean labour. No wonder that she sometimes shrinks from the task and joins the company of timid, lazy women who do not want to vote. But she *must* manage her home; for, no matter how grievously incompetent she may be, there is no one else authorized or able to manage it for her. She *must* secure for her children clean food at honest prices. Through all the changes of industry and government she remains the baker of bread, the minister of the universal sacrament of life.

When she demands to be mistress of the national granary, the national kitchen, the national dairy, the national sewing-room, whoever tells her to confine herself to her house is asking her to move forward and backward at the same time. This is a feat which even her inconsistency cannot achieve. The inconsistencies reside not in woman and her relation to her plain duties, but in her circumstances and in some of her critics. She can put a basket on her arm and bargain intelligently with a corner grocer; but she cannot understand the problem of nationalizing the railroads which have brought the food to the grocer's shop. She is clever at selecting a cut of meat; but the central meat-market must not be opened to her investigation; a congressional committee, which she did not choose, is doing its whole duty as father of the house when it tries to find out who owns the packing-houses in Chicago, how much money the owners make out of her dinner, and why thousands of tons of meat are shipped out of the country while her family is hungry.

She opens a can of food which is adulterated with worthless or dangerous stuff. In a distant city a man is building himself a palace with the profits of many such cans. If a petty thief should break into her pantry, and she should fight him tooth and nail, she would be applauded for her spirit and bravery; but when a millionaire manufacturer a thousand miles away robs her by the peaceful methods of commerce, she has nothing to say, because she does not understand business, and politics is not for her to meddle in.

Woman's old "domestic sphere" has become not only an empty shell with much of the contents removed, but a fragile shell in which she is not safe. Beside her own hearth she may be poisoned, starved, and robbed. When shall we have done with the tyranny which applies worn-out formulas to modern conditions? When shall we learn that domestic economy is political economy? The noblest task of woman is to get bread for her children. Whatever touches her children's bread is her business.

Woman from times long gone has been the nurse, the consoler, the healer of pain. To-day the sick-bed is often in a great public hospital. There she has followed it as professional nurse, and her services have been welcomed and acknowledged. In the hospital wards where she moves, deft, cheerful, capable, there are men unnecessarily laid low by the accidents of trade, and children maimed and dying who might be well and playing merrily in the bright morning of life. From the battlefields of industry come the wounded, from the shambles of poverty come the deformed. What enemy has stricken them? How much of all this disease and misery is preventable? Shall the wise nurse stand by the bed of pain and ask no questions about the social causes of ill-health? If her own child in her own home is needlessly hurt, she blames herself for her carelessness. In the world-home if a child is needlessly hurt, she is equally responsible. By her vigilance in the world-home woman can help to bring about a civilization in which every preventable disease shall be rooted out, and every condition that causes broken bodies shall be examined and abolished. This is her problem. She is mistress of the sick-room, and the sick-room is world-wide.

The education of children is acknowledged as lying within the scope of maternal care. The mother is the first teacher before the child goes to school, and in the schoolroom her unmarried sister devotes herself as a professional foster-mother to the children of others. The American nursery is a public building with a flag flying over it. If anywhere, woman is mistress in the schoolroom. So evident is this that in relation to schools she has a certain political privilege. She can vote for the school committee and serve on it herself. But even here she is bound by a very short tether. She has nothing official to say about how much money shall be spent for schools. Her freedom in this respect, as in some others, is the form without the substance. For the fundamental question in the public school problem is the question of money. Money must be appropriated by men. Moreover, the laws relating to children, for example, the laws of compulsory education, are made by men. It is not for her to say whether a child shall be taken from school to grind in mill and factory. Yet every child plunged in ignorance, bent by man's work before his time, is a thwarting of her sacred mission to fill the world with children well-born, well-bred, beautiful, wise, strong for the burdens of life! The schoolroom and all that it means belongs to the central intimacy of home, and all that violates the schoolroom violates the sanctity of the woman's hearth.

It is idle to say that woman could not improve the schools, that the schools are already free, and that every child has opportunity for instruction. The efficiency of the school depends upon things outside the schoolroom. It has been found that you must feed your child before you can teach it, and that the poor home defeats the best schoolroom. Behind the free school we must have a free people. What profits it to provide costly school buildings for anemic, under-fed children, to pass compulsory education laws and not secure a livelihood for the families whose children must obey them? What is the common sense of free text-books without wholesome food and proper clothing? Where is the logic — masculine or feminine — of free schools and free child-labour in the same commonwealth? These questions concern the most ignorant woman and the best educated woman, and the solution of them is necessary to the health and comfort of every home.

Woman's place is still the household. But the household is more spacious than in times gone by. Not all the changes of modern life have changed woman's duties essentially. Her work as spinner, bread-giver, helper of the helpless, mother and teacher of children is nowise different to-day but is immensely increased and intensified. Too often confused by the dazzle and uproar of modern life, she is the primal woman still, the saviour and shaper of the race.

In what a grim, strange abode must she often discharge her old-time functions! Sometimes it is no home at all, but an overcrowded, sunless lodging; it is not a shelter, but an industrial prison; it is not a nursery, but a lazaretto. Countless mothers of men have no place fit to be born in, to bear others in, to die in. Packed in tenements forgot of light, unheeded and slighted, starved of eye and ear and heart, they wear out their dull existence in monotonous toil — all for a crust of bread! They strive and labour, sweat and produce; they subject their bodies and soul i to every risk, lest their children die for want of food. Their clever hands which have so long been set to the spindle and the distaff, their patience, their industry, their cheapness, have but served to herd them in masses under the control of a growing industrial despotism.

Why is all this? Partly because woman does not own and direct her own share of the national household. True government is nothing but the management of this household for the good of the family. Under what kind of government do we live? To this question, her question, woman must find an answer by following her sisters to their places of sojourn. It is for her to know if their home is home indeed, if their shelter is strong and healthful, if every room — in lodging, shop, and factory — is open to light and air. It is for her to see that every dweller therein has freedom to drink in the winds of heaven and refresh his mind with music, art, and books; it is for her to see that every mother is enabled to bring up her children under favourable circumstances.

The greatest change is coming that has ever come in the history of the world. Order is evolving out of the chaos that followed the breaking up of the old system in which each household lived after its own manner. By using the physical forces of the universe men have replaced the slow hand-processes with the swift power of machines. If women demand it, a fair share of the machine-products will go to them and their families, as when the loom stood at hand in their dwellings. They will no more give all their best years to keep bright and fair the homes of others while their own are neglected. They will no more consume all their time, strength, and mental capacity in bringing up the rosy, laughing children of others while their own sweet children grow up pitiful and stunted. There is motherhood enough in the world to go round if it is not abused and wasted.

Yes, the greatest change is coming that has ever come in the history of the world. The idea that a higher power decrees definite stations for different human beings — that some are born to be kings and others to be slaves — is passing away. We know that there is plenty of room in the world and plenty of raw material in it for us all to be born right, to be brought up right, to work right, and to die right. We know that by the application of ordinary intelligence and common good-will, we can secure to every one of our children the means of culture, progress, and knowledge, of reasonable comfort, health, and happiness, or, if not happiness, at least freedom from the unnecessary misery which we all suffer to-day. This is the new faith that is taking the place of the faith in blind, selfish, capricious powers. Religion, the life of which is to do good, is supplanting the old servile superstitions. The spirit of the time we are in has been eloquently described by Henry Demarest Lloyd:

"It is an ethical renaissance, and insists that the divine ideals preached for thousands of years by the priests of humanity be put into form, now, here, and practically, in farm and mine, stock-market, factory, and bank. It denies point-blank that business is business. It declares business to be business and politics and religion. Business is the stewardship of the commissary of mankind, the administration of the resources upon which depend the possibilities of the human life, which is the divine life."

What is there, then, so cold, sordid, inhuman in economics that we women should shrink from the subject, disclaim all part in it, when we touch it daily in our domestic lives?

Many young women full of devotion and good-will have been engaged in superficial charities. They have tried to feed the hungry without knowing the causes of poverty. They have tried to minister to the sick without understanding the cause of disease. They have tried to raise up fallen sisters without knowing the brutal arm of necessity that struck them down. We give relief to a mother here and there, and still women are worn out at their daily tasks. We attempt social reforms where we need social transformations. We mend small things and leave the great things untouched. We strive after order and comfort in a few households, regardless of the world where distress prevails and loveliness is trodden in the dust.

Our abiding-place will be home indeed when the world outside is a peaceful, bright home for mankind. Woman's happiness depends upon her knowledge of the facts of life as much as upon her lovely thoughts and sweet speech and her faithfulness to small duties. In woman is wrapped the hope of the future. The new child, the new civilization, all the possibilities that sleep in mankind are enfolded in her. In her travail is the resurrection of the human race. All this glorious promise can be brought to naught by ignorance of the world in which it is to be fulfilled. To plead with woman to urge her to open her eyes to the great affairs of life, is merely to bid her make ready her house for the child that is to be born.

An Apology for Going to College

McClure's Magazine; June, 1905.

Five years ago I had to decide whether I should be a heretic, or adhere to the ancient faith that it is the woman's part to lay her hands to the spindle and to hold the distaff. Some of my friends were enthusiastic about the advantages of a college education, and the special honour it would be for me to compete with my fellows who see and hear. Others were doubtful. One gentleman said to me: "I do not approve of college women, because they lose all respect for men." This argument had, however, the opposite effect to what was intended; for I thought if our respect for men could be philosophized, or economized, or debated, or booked away, or by any learning rendered null and void, the men must be at fault, and it was my duty as a woman to try to reestablish them on their ancient pedestal. Fortunately women are born with a missionary spirit.

The champions of what Bacon calls "she-colleges," gave their persuasions a Baconian turn. "College maketh a full man; conference a ready man; and writing an exact man, and so," said they, "college maketh a full, ready, and exact woman." If I did not confer, I should have a hoar-frost on my wits, and if I did not read under judicious instruction, I should have to pretend to knowledge in the presence of Princess Ida and her "violet-hooded doctors." Then came yet other people who set to work to destroy the arguments of the advocates. "What use is there in your going to college? You will find much drudgery, and you must renounce many of your dearest pleasures. What will come of it? You cannot hope to teach or turn your education to practical account. Why not take life pleasantly? Why not stay at home and read books and develop your individuality? College is only for mediocre people, not for geniuses." (This was music in my fingers!) It grieves me that those who spoke so eloquently should have spoken in vain. But love of knowledge had stopped the ears with which I hear. I felt that all the forces of my nature were cudgelling me to college. It was not in the hope of large scholarship that I made the pilgrimage to this laborious Eldorado. (The riches I sought consisted in learning to do something, and do it well. I felt, and still feel, that the demand of the world is not so much for scholarship as for effective serviced The world needs men and women who are able to work, and who will work with enthusiasm; and it is to college graduates that this nation has a right to look for intelligent sons and daughters who will return to the State tenfold what the State has given to them.

I realized that the avenues of usefulness opened to me were few and strait. But who shall set bounds to the aspirations of the mind, or limit that which the Lord hath created in His mercy and goodness? I had a mind to begin with, and two good hands by which I had groped my way to the frontiers of knowledge. Beyond the frontiers there might be stretches of desert; but if you must pass through a desert to reach the smiling land of plenty, set forth bravely, and the hard journey across the waste places shall give strength to your feet. We derive benefit from the things we do not like, but do nevertheless because they have to be done, and done all the more conscientiously because we do not like them. Necessity teaches patience and obedience.

These considerations, then, determined me to take a college course. I suppose I appeared to many of my advisers like the Philistines who went to the wars as men proud of destruction. People are too prone to think that the actual is the limit of possibility. They believe that all that has been done is all that can be done. They ridicule every departure from practice. "No deaf - blind person has ever taken a college course," they say. "Why do you attempt what no one else has ventured? Even if you succeed in passing the entrance examinations, you cannot go on after you get into college. You have no books. You cannot hear lectures. You cannot make notes. You are most foolhardy to attempt something in which you are sure to fail." Thus counselled the unadventurous people to whom the untrodden field is full of traps and pitfalls. Although they are Christians, yet they are possessed of the idea that man does everything, and God does nothing! The argument brought against me, that no deaf-blind person had ever gone to college, was precisely the kind of argument brought a generation ago against any woman's going to college. True, there had been seminaries and academies for girls, but no colleges of a university standard; and the so-called universities for men showed stern oaken doors to all women. There was no precedent for trying woman's intelligence in a fair contest by the high criterion men had established for themselves: but women created a new precedent.

Before 1878, women, backed by public opinion, were already standing at the door of Harvard demanding higher education, and conservative men felt uneasy lest they should seem selfishly to monopolize knowledge. A few progressive members of the Harvard Faculty agreed to teach women in private classes. There was a precedent for this; for in England women were already receiving instruction from professors of Oxford and Cambridge. The new project in American Cambridge enlisted, between 1879 and 1881, the services of nearly forty Harvard instructors. According to an historian, the few women who availed themselves of this new opportunity were keen, earnest, and capable to such a degree that the only trouble was to satisfy their demands. In 1882 the Society for the Collegiate Instruction of Women was organized. The next year three young women finished the four years' course, and about fifty were taking partial courses. All had proved their ability to do work at least equal to that of Harvard students. Yet there were no degrees to reward them, only certificates stating that the course they had taken was equal to one at Harvard. Even when Atalanta won the race, the prize went still to a lame Hippomenes!

In 1894 the Society took the name of Radcliffe College, and got its charter from the legislature, which gave it the right to confer its own degree. This degree is countersigned by the president of Harvard, who warrants it equal to a Harvard degree. We owe Radcliffe not to Harvard, but to the success of those first earnest students who proved that they were able to do university work, and to the large-minded professors who, by unofficial and individual devotion to learning, helped the pilgrim band to found a safe, permanent home where other women could come. That little band has transmitted the torch of learning for women from frontier to frontier, until there is not a State in the Union which does not provide for the higher education of women. Every woman, whether she can go to college or not, owes a great deal to those pioneers who cleared a place in the wilderness of men's prejudice for the lowly walls of the first woman's college.

Radcliffe College was a new and stronger expression of the spirit which had founded several good American colleges for girls. For the first time in America women's educational opportunities were equal to those of men.

Radcliffe College inherits the spirit of the women who, twenty-seven years ago, sought knowledge for its own sake. Radcliffe is still for earnest women who seek knowledge for its own sake. Girls who go there should have some object in view, some standard of excellence, the gift of handling knowledge in a plain, downright way. There is too little teaching at Harvard and Radcliffe, but there is much opportunity to learn. You may take the treasures offered, or leave them. At Radcliffe, I think, the treasures are more highly valued than among the young gentlemen across the street; for young men, I am told, go to college for a variety of reasons, or for no reason at all. A girl who goes to Radcliffe should be filled with the desire to look behind the forms of things into things themselves, and to add to beauty and softness, solidity and accuracy of knowledge. Stucco is no more serviceable to woman than to man. A well-trained mind and the ability to grasp the ideas essential to a purpose and carry them out with perseverance — this is the ideal Radcliffe places before women. How far this ideal can be realized appeared at a meeting of Radcliffe alumnae last year, where there were nine speakers — the scholar, the poet, the teacher, the dramatist, the administrative woman, the woman in domestic life. Their success had lain in different directions, and each testified that she owed her success in large part to her training at Radcliffe. Any young woman who acquires the self-control which Radcliffe teaches, and performs her task resolutely, may stand up before the kings of learning and not be ashamed, whether she be a writer, a teacher, a speaker, an administrative woman, a society woman, or a home-maker, Radcliffe strives to give her students the substance of wisdom, and to promote earnest and independent scholarship. In her, discipline, knowledge, and self-mastery have replaced the narrow rules of conduct and the prudish dogmatism of the old-fashioned women's academies, just as arbitration and statesmanship are replacing the soldier and the priest. If the classes at Radcliffe which sit under Professor Kittredge and Doctor Royce are not learned, they at least carry away with them a sense of the dignity of scholarship, and do not, like Becky Sharp, when they depart through the college gate, hurl Johnson's dictionary at their preceptor's head.

For the first time in the history of the world, women are expected to have an intelligent understanding of business, of politics, of all the practical problems of our modern life. The college woman learns to cooperate with others, and that means she learns how not to have her own way. Experience in college activities teaches her the right of her companions to freedom of thought and action. By throwing herself into college affairs, she acquires the habit of rendering intelligent and efficient service to others; so that when she graduates, she becomes a practical force in the world, and a responsible member of society.

Like all human institutions Radcliffe falls short of her ideals, and her students, who are also human, do not always achieve theirs. I am acquainted with one who did not. Where I failed, the fault was sometimes my own, sometimes attributable to the peculiar circumstances under which I worked.

But my successes were made possible by the spirit and the methods of the college and its unique advantages. And there were many advantages I could not avail myself of. The lectures, libraries, theatres, and museums for which Boston and Cambridge are celebrated, and which largely supplement college work, were not of service to me. The advantages of especial value to me were the excellence of the instruction and the liberality of the elective system. The quality of the instruction at Radcliffe is beyond question; for it is given by the best men at Harvard. The elective system offers a broad variety of courses and freedom of choice. Many subjects were impossible for me on account of my limitations, and I could not have planned my course so as to win a degree but for the scope of the Radcliffe curriculum. The ordinary student, who is not so restricted as I was, has wider opportunities, and she must choose wisely. In her very selection of courses there is a chance to "develop her individuality." And in the exercise of judgment as to the amount of time and energy she will devote to her work, she proves her individuality.

In a college like Radcliffe, where so much depends on individual judgment, students fall naturally into three classes: first, those who choose their course wisely and pursue it with consistency, without sacrificing other joys and interests; second, "joyless grinds" who study for high marks; and third, those who choose indiscriminately courses that are pleasant, easy, and unrelated.

In the first class are those who realize that to get the greatest benefit from college it is necessary to take one's time, to proceed at an easy gait, and not to hurry or scramble. They know the pleasure of lingering over a subject, of asking questions, and of following an idea as fancy listeth. Happy study is as sweet to the true student as news of his sweetheart to the ardent lover. But the happy following of an interesting idea is not always possible. The arbitrary demands of instructors and the exigencies of a mechanical routine often forbid it. If my college is at fault in not permitting enough leisurely and meditative study, I hereby suggest my panacea — fewer courses, and more time for each.

Every student has a panacea for some weakness of his alma mater. One would have dull professors prohibited, another would have all dates and formulas weeded out, another would have examinations abolished, another would do away with daily themes extorted from impoverished minds — a most tyrannical oppression, taxation without representation, the wrong which lost England her thirteen colonies! If the instructors would only consult the benevolent, reforming student, he could give them Valuable points. But instead of consulting the student's profound intuitions, the instructors go forward in a straight, narrow line, never looking to the right or to the left, blind and deaf to the wisdom that crieth on the campus. The younger the student is, the more confident he is that he has found the solution of the problem. He often forgets that his alma mater has given him the very wisdom with which he sharpens his darts against her. The critical student sees that the reformative schemes of his fellow-students are valueless. Their incompetence is glaring! But as he grows older he sees his own folly too. If after his graduation he has tried to plan the curriculum of a small primary school and failed, he too will turn conservative, and leave to time's slow evolution the great problems of education.

To be candid, I have proposed the leisurely, reflective manner of study because I have an indolent, wayward mind which likes to ramble through the garden of knowledge, picking here a leaf, there a blossom, and so off to pastures new. Fortunately, the spirit of Radcliffe and a good conscience forbid that the student shall abuse her liberties. It is good for us to read books we do not like. The performance of set tasks and work that is not of our choosing are stimulating. Miry ways and rugged mountain-paths mean strength, grit, poise. If they draw out our miles and make them wearisome, it only means that we have new vigour added to us, and that we shall enter into the treasures of endurance. I know not whether I with more delight strapped the knapsack over my shoulder, or set it down at the end of the journey. The mastering of difficulties is followed by a sense of wellbeing and capacity which is like a river of water in a dry land, like a shadow of a great rock in the heat.

The girl who is not a slave to books, who selects her courses judiciously and gives them a right and proper amount of strength, is not to be confounded with the girl whose independence is mere indifference or egotism. Not such do I admire, and, for all my pet schemes to reform my college, not such am I. I only maintain that we have a right to ourselves, that we should be masters of our books and preserve our serenity. There is no profit where there is no pleasure. College consists of five parts sense and five parts what, from the class-room point of view, would be called nonsense; but nonsense is the very vitality of youth. After all, book-knowledge is not the most important thing to acquire, and perpetual work on five or six courses cannot be sustained without neglect of other important things. Even thoughtful and independent girls try to do so much that they can do nothing thoroughly. They rush, cram, thieve many hours from their nights, and for all their ill-timed industry they hand in next morning papers full of mistakes. Although I always tried to work with a cool head and steady hand, and sleep according to the law, I, too, was drawn into this whirlpool of confused, incomplete tasks. I met other girls in the college halls and on the stairs who stopped a moment to greet me, but they were rushing from lecture to examination, from examination to basket-ball practice, from practice to dramatic rehearsal, from rehearsal to conference, and there was no time for a pleasant chat. And if the girls who had eyes and ears were overburdened and distraught, I was at least no better off. During four years a torrent of miscellaneous knowledge poured through my fingers, and it fills me with despair to think how much of the choicest matter of this abundant stream dripped and oozed away. I was eager to draw from the living waters of wisdom; but my pitcher must have had a hole in it. I was like the Danaides who poured water eternally into a broken urn.

Once in a while a book or an instructor started a vein of bright thoughts. I caught a glimpse of old truths in a new perspective; but I could not linger. Before I had got a good look, I was hurried away on the current of words, and in the effort to keep from being upset in midstream I lost sight of the bright idea, and on reaching firm ground I was chagrined to find that it had fallen overboard. The idea thus irrevocably lost was often one on which depended a fortnightly composition, or even a three hours' examination. I was of course hampered by my limitations, which turned to drudgery much work that might have been delightful; for they imposed upon me tedious methods of study. I was often behind in my work at a distance forbidden by military law; I was never ahead; and once I fell so far behind that it seemed as if I might as well try to keep pace with a shooting star! Experience, however, taught me to tack against wind and tide — the first lesson of life I learned in college. And this was easier with Miss Sullivan at the helm. I would not part with one of those struggles against the gales — "the winds and persecutions of the sky." They tested my powers and developed the individuality which I had been advised to bring up on books at home.

Had I not gone to college, I should have missed some of the authors whose individuality taught me to value my own without isolating myself from the seeing and hearing world. I discovered that darkness and silence might be rich in possibilities, which in my turn I might discover to the world. In other words, I found the treasures of my own island. For that I am largely indebted to Professor Charles T. Copeland, my instructor in English composition.

Different students seek different treasures. To some the most precious nuggets are high marks. Such plodders as I watch their quest from afar. We hear about them with the wonder with which we listened to the fairy tales of our childhood; but we should not dream of following them any more than we should think of going in search of the singing-tree in the "Arabian Nights." Their high marks are no incentive to us to fill our midnight lamps with oil that we may enter in with the wise virgins. They stuff themselves with dates, and with figs gathered of thistles, and think themselves blessed. They have dyspeptic nightmares of the brain, in which they go through flood and fire, seeking the phantom gold at the rainbow's end.

The court to which they return from a futile quest, or with meagre spoil, is a chamber of inquisition. Oh, the examinations! They separate us from our kind. They water our pillows, they drive sleep from our beds, they inspire us with hope, then dash us ruthlessly from our pinnacle, they cross-question us until their martyrs lie in the dust, and their apostasy is the open secret of the universe. Oh, those little crisp sheets of paper written with a pencil of fire which consumeth ideas like chaff! They are the accidents of time and flesh, they are mere conundrums on which we throw away our beauty sleep; and, in the end, all the dull substance of our brains and our ingenious padding dwindle to a lame and impotent conclusion.

Before an examination we feel delightfully precocious and original. After it we are full of the wise things we did not say. We took twice as much trouble as was necessary to prepare our subject only to miss the essential points after all. The least explicable thing that an examination paper does is to destroy your sense of proportion and reduce everything you have read to a dead level. Like Doctor Johnson you make your little fishes talk like whales, and your whales twitter like canary birds, and the result is a collision of contrary absurdities!

The chief loss of a girl who "grinds" is that she misses other college activities. It is the light of college education to join with one's fellow-students on class-teams, in college plays, and on the college magazines. For the most part you study by yourself; but in the united activities of class and college you learn the tact and community which are the beginning of useful service to mankind. Of course I had little part in the social life of my college. I enjoyed my share of work; the obstacles which were declared insurmountable came against me one way and retreated seven ways, and that was happiness enough. I had, too, many pleasures, solitary and apart from the other girls, but as genuine as theirs. They often invited me to join their frolics and club-meetings, and it cost me many a twinge of regret not to be able to take part in their affairs; for I was keenly alive to everything that interested them. If I had been of the class of 1906 or 1907, I should have met them oftener in the new Elizabeth Cary Agassiz House, which is to be the social centre of Radcliffe, and I should have felt the inspiration of their activities. Nothing encourages us so much as the example of others, nothing stirs our energies more than generous emulation, nothing comforts us so much in discouragement as companionship. My friendships must come through the medium of my hand, and few of the girls knew the manual alphabet; and the conditions under winch we shook hands for a moment in the crowded class-room were not favourable to intimacy. They could not reach me through my illation, and in the midst of my class I could not help at times feeling lonely and sad.

But a happy disposition turns everything to good, yea, the want of one thing, lacking which so many melancholy beings want everything. I forgot my loneliness in the cheerful realities that touched me. I knew there was a rich store of experience outside my comprehension, but the little I could grasp was wonderful enough, and having contentment I was possessed of the boon whereof I had been beggared.

A happy spirit is worth a library of learning. I think I derived from the daily walk to college with Miss Sullivan more genuine pleasure than comes to many a girl who sits in a corner and works the sunshine, the fresh air, and even good humour out of her morning lessons — all for high marks.

On the other hand, I do not understand the motives of that third class of girls who go to college, apparently, to be entertained. I do not see the use of studies chosen from year to year, without plan or forethought, because this instructor marks easily, or that professor is "so nice," or the conference man is "so polite," or "Doctor G. keeps you so interested" — in himself, that means, not in the subject. These girls dip into all that treats of whatsoever is, the state, the total chronicle of man, chemical and electrical laws, and whatsoever can be taught and known. "General education" is their apology, their rock of defence, their tabernacle from which they shall not be moved. I have known girls who graduated, and with good marks, too, whose minds seemed to me undisciplined and crammed with odds and ends of knowledge which they displayed for the enlightenment of their friends. They reminded me of the maidens of old whose accomplishments were feminine and elegant, who brought out a sketch-book to be inspected by admiring friends. The sketches represented nothing that creepeth on the ground, flieth in the air or passeth through the paths of the seas, but they were ladylike all the same. Girls whose education is too general shall prove to have none at all. Their infinite variety will be withered by age and staled by custom.

The ideal of college education is not to give miscellaneous instruction, but to disclose to the student his highest capacities and teach him how to turn them to achievement. By this ideal, those who labour in darkness are brought to see a great light, and those who dwell in silence shall give service in obedience to the voice of love.

To the New College Girl

Youth's Companion, June 8, 1905.

You have come up out of the primary school, through the grammar school, through the high school, and this beautiful June morning finds you standing where the brook meets the river.

The carefree days of childhood are past, and the mystery of an unknown life awaits you at the threshold of the college which you will enter next September.

It is fitting that you pause, serious and thoughtful; for you have not passed this way heretofore. The time has come when you must put away, with loving hands, the playthings of your childhood, the familiar habits and immunities and companions of your protected girlhood, leave solicitous friends and guardians, and enter, through the college door, upon the larger responsibilities and joys of womanhood. Your life is before you, "so various, so beautiful, so new."

The power and the delight of unknown coming things are filling your minds with glad expectancy. You are ready to walk erect and fearless in the ways of knowledge. You have resolved to go to college, and you stand prepared to make your resolution a living fact, a visible bodying forth of the purpose that is in you. But you must first lay aside anxiety of mind and distrust of your powers; for knowledge is holy ground, and joy alone shall lead your steps aright.

It is often said that usefulness is the end of life; and so it is. But happiness creates and inspires usefulness. If you have many gifts, and the power to understand, even if you meditate night and day how to promote the welfare of the world, it shall all profit you little if you have not joy. Take up joy, then, as you stand before the gate of your student life, and enter fearlessly. Think that the college you have set your hearts on holds all good things in her hand. Believe that in her halls your higher dreams shall be realized. But do not forget that the great gifts which you are about to receive from your college bring with them great obligations, and that your larger freedom is a sacred bondage to great ideas.

In college you will be brought face to face with nearly all the fundamental questions of life, and you will learn how many men have tried to solve them. Hitch your wagon to a happy star, and you also shall help to solve them. The world needs your intellect, your scholarship, but most of all your hearts — hearts that are loving, brave, hopeful, happy.

Does all this dream of high privilege and noble service seem far above your circumstances, beyond the reach of your strength and your powers of mind? Remember what Senator Hoar said: "Much of the good work of the world has been that of dull people who have done their best." Many a girl who thought herself mediocre has won high honours in college.

Fears and regrets have no place in the vocabulary of youth, whose spirit sets its white and shining wings toward the purple shores of the Promised Land. Be happy, talk happiness. Happiness calls out responsive gladness in others. There is enough sadness in the world without yours. Rebel against the hardness and injustice of things as much as you like. It is always well to keep your fighting edge keen to smite wrongs wherever you meet them. But never doubt the excellence and permanence of what is yet to be. Never doubt that this is God's world, and that it is brought nearer to Him by the right work of the least of His children no less than by the mighty works of genius. You are no less necessary to the world's uplifting than Luther and Lincoln.

Join the great company of those who make the barren places of life fruitful with kindness. Carry a vision of heaven in your souls, and you shall make your home, your college, the world correspond to that vision. Your success and happiness lie in you. External conditions are the accidents of life, its outer trappings. The great, enduring realities are love and service. Joy is the holy fire that keeps our purpose warm and our intelligence aglow. Work without joy shall be as nothing. Resolve to keep happy, and your joy and you shall form an invincible host against difficulties.

Perhaps in college you may meet with books which suggest to you that it is noble and comely to be unhappy. Many clever people have found many reasons for unhappiness. Some learned men have peered between the curtains of life's tabernacle, found it empty and a cunning sham, and in the dimness of their spiritual sight they have gone away grumbling, never suspecting their own blindness. From their conclusions turn to Stevenson and Browning, read St. Paul's epistles, learn that the tabernacle is a temple wherein God abides.

Think, read, study diligently day by day, and the severest tests of your knowledge shall find you prepared and confident. Do not lose sleep over the prospect of examinations, or fret above the printed page until you cannot read its lessons clear. Even if you do not win academic distinction, remember that it may be more worth while to help another girl perform a difficult task than to win a high mark yourself. It is less important to do justice to books than to be honest and kind and generous in your relations to your fellow-students.

Face your deficiencies and acknowledge them; but do not let them master you. Let them teach you patience, sweetness, insight. True education combines intellect, beauty, goodness, and the greatest of these is goodness. When we do the best that we can, we never know what miracle is wrought in our life, or in the life of another.

To go to college is like going to a strange town to live. Your fellow-students are of all sorts and classes, and often seem to have nothing in common with each other, except the desire for approbation, sympathy, and love. If you understand the complex diversity of a college community, you will be spared many disappointments in your freshman year. When you find yourselves forlorn and homesick for a time, you will not feel bitterly toward the other girls because they do not follow you about the campus, or stop you on the stairs to offer you their undying friendship.

The freshman is often painfully aware of qualities of mind and heart which should place her high in the council of her class, and she is surprised that others are so slow to recognize them. But you will find your place in college as surely as water seeks its level. Only you must not sit and mope, or stand outside your class and criticise its officers, athletics, and clubs. You must throw yourselves into the midst of its activities and discover where you can be useful. To be a leader in your class requires the same qualities that are required to be a leader anywhere. It is not so much genius that availeth as energy, industry, and willingness to make personal sacrifices.

Learn from your books not only the day's lesson, but the life lesson. In all knowledge, in the classics, in science, in history and literature, and in mathematics you will see the struggle of man to get nearer to God. Resolve, then, as you stand on the threshold of your student days, with an enlightened optimism to consecrate your education to the service of others. When your thoughts become pessimistic, when it seems as if all men were deafened by the tumult of trade, blinded by self-interest and greed turn the pages of your history of England, and you will find that the ideas which shaped the Anglo-Saxon race were not mean or sordid.

American history, too, is filled with heroes and martyrs who joyfully pushed aside ambition and gave their lives to the common weal.

"Are men blind?" they cried. "We will open their eyes. Are they deaf? We will unstop their ears. Are they hungry? They shall be fed. Are they cast down and oppressed? As God liveth, they shall be free!"

The world needs more of this spirit of service. There is still many a desert place where the sun of love and the light of truth have not shone. The occasion waits for every college graduate, in the joyous erectness of youth, and vigour, to answer, "Lord, here am I; send me."

Letter to an English Woman-Suffragist

Published in the Manchester (England) *Advertiser,* March 3, 1911.

I thank you for the copy of "Votes for Women." Mr. Zangwill's address interested me deeply. You ask me to comment on it, and though I know little, your request encourages me to tell you some of my ideas on the subject.

I have thought much lately about the question of woman-suffrage, and I have followed in my Braille magazines the recent elections in Great Britain. The other day I read a fine report of an address by Miss Pankhurst at a meeting in New York.

I do not believe that the present government has any intention of giving woman a part in national politics, or of doing justice to Ireland, or to the workmen of England. So long as the franchise is denied to a large number of those who serve and benefit the public, so long as those who vote are at the beck and call of party machines, the people are not free, and the day of women's freedom seems still to be in the far future. It makes no difference whether the Tories or the Liberals in Great Britain, the Democrats or the Republicans in the United States, or any party of the old model in any other country get the upper hand. To ask any such party for women's rights is like asking a czar for democracy.

Are not the dominant parties managed by the ruling classes, that is, the propertied classes, solely for the profit and privilege of the few? They use us millions to help them into power. They tell us like so many children that our safety lies in voting for them. They toss us crumbs of concession to make us believe that they are working in our interest. Then they exploit the resources of the nation not for us, but for the interests which they represent and uphold. We, the people, are not free. Our democracy is but a name. We vote? What does that mean? It means that we choose between two bodies of real, though not avowed autocrats. We choose between Tweedledum and Tweedledee. We elect expensive masters to do our work for us, and then blame them because they work for themselves and for their class. The enfranchisement of women is a part of the vast movement to enfranchise all mankind. You ask for votes for women. What good can votes do you when ten elevenths of the land of Great Britain belongs to two hundred thousand, and only one eleventh to the rest of the forty millions? Have your men with their millions of votes freed themselves from this injustice?

When one shows the masters that half the wealth of Great Britain belongs to twenty-five thousand persons, when one says that this is wrong, that this wrong lies at the bottom of all social injustice, including the wrongs of women, the highly respectable newspapers cry, "Socialist agitator, stirrer of class strife!" Well, let us agitate, let us confess that we are thoroughgoing Social Democrats or anything else that they please to label us. But let us keep our eyes on the central fact, that a few, a few British men own the majority of British men and all British women. The few own the many because they possess the means of livelihood of all. In our splendid republic, where at election time all are "free and equal," a few Americans own the rest. Eighty per cent, of our people live in rented houses, and one half the rest are mortgaged. The country is governed for the richest, for the corporations, the bankers, the land speculators, and for the exploiters of labour. Surely we must free men and women together before we can free women.

The majority of mankind are working people. So long as their fair demands — the ownership and control of their lives and livelihood — are set at naught, we can have neither men's rights nor women's rights. The majority of mankind are ground down by industrial oppression in order that the small remnant may live in ease. How can women hope to help themselves while we and our brothers are helpless against the powerful organizations which modern parties represent, and which contrive to rule the people? They rule the people because they own the means of physical life, land, and tools, and the nourishers of intellectual life, the press, the church, and the school. You say that the conduct of the woman suffragists is being disgracefully misrepresented by the British press. Here in America the leading newspapers misrepresent in every possible way the struggles of toiling men and women who seek relief. News that reflects ill upon the employers is skillfully concealed — news of dreadful conditions under which labourers are forced to produce, news of thousands of men maimed in mills and mines and left without compensation, news of famines and strikes, news of thousands of women driven to a life of shame, news of little children compelled to labour before their hands are ready to drop their toys. Only here and there in a small and as yet uninfluential paper is the truth told about the workman and the fearful burdens under which he staggers.

I am indignant at the treatment of the brave, patient women of England. I am indignant when the women cloakmakers of Chicago are abused by the police. I am filled with anguish when I think of the degradation, the enslavement and the industrial tyranny which crush millions, and drag down women and helpless children,

I know the deep interest which you and your husband always took in God's poor, and your sympathy invites me to open my heart to you and express these opinions about grave problems.

How to Become a Writer

A letter to a blind boy. Printed in the World's Work, April. 1910.

Your letter interested me very much, and I would gladly tell you how to become a writer if I knew. But alas! I do not know how to become one myself. No one can be taught to write. One can learn to write if he has it in him; but he does not learn from a teacher, counsellor, or adviser. No education, however careful and wise, will furnish talent. It only gives material to one who has talent to work with. If I could explain the process and command the secrets of this strange elusive faculty, the first thing I should do would be to write the greatest novel of the century, an epic and a volume of sonnets thrown in. I should at once set about making great writers of some hundreds and thousands of Americans. I should "stump" the States and get bills passed for the promotion of high-grade literature. I should see to it that among our national products authors with noble powers had the chief place.

I believe the only place to look for the information you desire is in the biographies of successful authors. As far as I know, one fact is common to them all. In their youth they read good books and began writing in a simple way. They kept the best models of style before them. They played with words until they could criticise their own compositions and strike out dull or badly managed passages. They journeyed on, now taking a step forward, impelled by the desire to write, now at a standstill, held back by defects of style or lack of ideas. One day they wrote a real book, they awoke to find that they had a literary gift - the idea had come, and they were prepared to express it! I would suggest that you read the autobiographies of Benjamin Franklin and Anthony Trollope. In these books the authors tell us, not how they learned to write — that was a thing not in their power to divulge — but what steps they took to improve their powers. And simple steps they are, such as you and I can follow, Mr. Macy's new book, "A Guide to Reading," may also be useful to you.

You see, there is but one road to authorship. It remains forever a way in which each man must go a-pioneering. The struggles of the pen may be as severe as those of the axe and hammer. One needs right mental eyes to discern the signs of talent which writers have left on their pages, like so many "blazes" upon trees in the forest. Well! I am not a novelist or a poet, I fear, and that metaphor is running away with me. What I mean is, we can follow where literary folk have gone; but, in order to be authors ourselves, to be followed, we must strike into a path where no one has preceded us. Before we publish anything, or set ourselves up as writers, we may imitate and even copy to our hearts' content, and when the time comes for us to send forth a message to the world, we shall have learned how to say it.

From your letter I judge that you do not read with your fingers. You can do this, and you ought to learn as soon as possible. You are indeed fortunate that your parents can read aloud to you. But there is danger in only hearing language, and never seeing or touching it. Your memory will do you all the more service if you have embossed words placed at your finger-ends. Then reading for yourself will give you a better sense of language, and a good sense of words is the very basis of style.

Our Duties to the Blind

Presented at the first annual meeting of the Massachusetts Association for Promoting the Interests of the Adult Blind, January 5, 1904, in Boston.

The annual meeting of this association gives us another opportunity to discuss among ourselves, and to present to the public, the needs and interests of the adult blind, and I am glad to avail myself of the opportunity. This question of helping the blind to support themselves has been near to my heart for many years, since long before the formation of this society. All I have learned on the subject in the books I have read, I have stored up in my mind against the day when I should be able to turn it to the use of my blind fellows. That day has come.

I have heard that some people think the views I am expressing on this subject, and indeed on all subjects, are not my own, but Miss Sullivan's. If you please, I do very often express Miss Sullivan's ideas, just as to the best of my ability I express ideas which I have been fortunate enough to gather from other wise sources — from the books I have read, from the friends with whom I talk, even from the poets, the prophets, and the sages. It is not strange that some of my ideas come from the wise one with whom I am most intimate and to whom I owe all that I am. I rejoice for myself and for you if Miss Sullivan's ideas are commingled with mine. The more on that account ought what I say to receive your respectful consideration; for Miss Sullivan is acquainted with the work of the blind and the work for the blind. She was blind once herself, and she spent six years in the Perkins Institution. She has since proved a successful teacher of the blind. Other teachers from all over the world have sought her out and exchanged views with her. So Miss Sullivan's ideas on the matter we have to consider are those of an expert. But may I venture to protest I have some ideas of my own? It is true I am still an undergraduate, and I have not had time to study the problems of the blind so deeply as I shall some day. I have, however, thought about these problems, and I know that the time is ripe, nay, it has long been ripe, to provide for the adult blind the means of self-support.

The blind are in three classes: first, blind children, who need a common school education; second, the aged and the infirm blind, who need to be tenderly cared for; third, the able-bodied blind, who ought to work. For the first class, blind children, this state has splendidly provided in that great two-million dollar school, the Perkins Institution. The second class, like all other people who are invalid and infirm, must be sheltered in the embrace of many public and private charities. For the third class, healthy adult blind, nothing adequate has been done in this state. They do not want to go to school and read books. They do not want to be fed and clothed and housed by other people. They want to work and support themselves. The betterment of this class is the object of our association. We ask that the State give the adult blind opportunity to earn their own living. We do not approve any system to pauperize them. We are not asking for them a degrading pension or the abstract glories of a higher education. We want them apprenticed to trades, and we want some organized method of helping them to positions after they have learned these trades.

Consider the condition of the idle adult blind from the point of view of their fellow-citizens, and from their own point of view. What sort of citizens are they now? They are a public or a private burden, a bad debt, an object of pitying charity, an economic loss. What we ask for them, in the name of Christian philanthropy, we ask equally on the ground of economic good sense. If there are three thousand adult blind in this Commonwealth who could be taught to work, and who are not working, to keep them alive means a burden of ten or twelve thousand dollars every seven days. If each of the three thousand could be taught to work and earn three dollars a week — surely a low figure — the State would obviously be twenty or twenty-five thousand dollars a week richer. At present the adult blind form a large class who are unremunerative and unprofitable.

Such they are from the point of view of the thoughtful citizen. What are they from their point of view?

Not merely are they blind — that can be borne — but they live in idleness, which is the crudest, least bearable misery that can be laid upon the human heart. No anguish is keener than the sense of helplessness and self-condemnation which overwhelms them when they find every avenue to activity and usefulness closed to them. If they have been to school, their very education makes their sorrow keener because they know all the more deeply what they have lost. They sit with folded hands as the weary days drag by. They remember the faces they used to see, and the objects of delight which made life good to live, and above all they dream of work that is more satisfying than all the learning, all the pleasures gained by man, work that unites the world in friendly association, cheers solitude, and is the balm of hurt minds. They sit in darkness thinking with pain of the past, and with dread of the future that promises no alleviation of their suffering. They think until they can think no more, and some of them become morbid. The monotony and loneliness of their lives is conceivable only to those who have similar deprivations. I have enjoyed the advantages of the blind who are taught. Yet, I used to feel unhappy many times, because it seemed as if my limitation would prevent me from taking an active part in the work of the world. Never did my heart ache more than when I thought I was not fit to be a useful member of society. Now I have found abundant work, and I ask for no other blessedness.

I have talked with blind students at the institutions for the blind, and I remember the distress and perplexity with which they considered how they should shift for themselves when they graduated. Many of them left school only to go back to poor, bare homes where they could find no means of self-support. For seven, ten or fourteen years they live in the midst of refined surroundings; they enjoy good books, good music, and the society of cultivated people. When their school days are over, they return to homes and conditions which they have outgrown. The institution that has educated them forgets them, unless, perchance, they have sufficient ability to fight their life-battle single-handed and come out victorious. Institutions are proud of successful graduates. Let us not forget the failures. What benefit do the graduates who fail in the struggle of adult life derive from an education which has not been of a kind that could be turned to practical account? From an economic point of view has the money invested in that education been invested wisely? To teach Latin and Greek and higher mathematics to blind pupils, and not to teach them to earn their bread, is to build a house entirely of stucco, without stones to the walls or rafters to the roof. I have received letters from educated blind people, who repeat the cry, "Give us work, or we perish," and their despair lies heavy on my heart.

It is difficult to get satisfactory statistics about the blind after they graduate from the institutions where they receive a book education, because little or no interest is shown in them after they leave school. It is still harder to get information about the blind who have lost their sight when they are too old to go to the existing institutions. But it is evident that only a small portion of the blind now support themselves. A prominent teacher of the blind is reported to have said that less than 8 per cent, of the entire blind population of the United States, even those who have been to schools for the blind, are self-supporting, and the percentage for the whole country will be higher than the percentage for this State; for Massachusetts is behind some states in industrial education for the blind. Others will give you the exact figures. But whether there are in Massachusetts one thousand or five thousand adult blind who might be taught to work, they are too many for us to have neglected so long.

It is difficult to understand how a State which was a pioneer in the education of the blind, and which boasts the Perkins Institution, could have so conspicuously failed to turn their education to account. Surely it is only an accidental division which has left one; side of the education of the blind in the sunlight where Doctor Howe placed it, and has left the other side in the dark. In spirit, all aspects of the education of the blind are one, and we can be sure that Doctor Howe, had he lived, would have been the leader of this movement, in which we are doing our little best. Indeed, I believe that he would long ago have rendered our labours unnecessary. Let us gratefully and lovingly render, in company with those who survive him, the honour that is his due. But since he is dead and cannot lead us, let us push forward, guided by what light we have. Wisdom did not die with Solomon. All knowledge about the needs and capabilities of the blind did not die with Doctor Howe. There is much to do which he did not live to achieve, or, it may even be, which he had not thought of.

The important fact remains that nothing of consequence has been done for the adult blind in Massachusetts since Doctor Howe's day. It was he who established the workshop for the adult blind in South Boston, in connection with the Perkins Institution, and that remains much as he left it. Two or three years ago, the State appropriated a small sum of money — five thousand dollars, I think — for travelling teachers, who visit the homes of blind persons too old to go to the Perkins Institution. This was a step in the right direction, but it was inadequate, and it is not altogether practical. I have known old ladies who have told me how glad they were to learn to read the Lord's Prayer with their fingers. They looked forward to the weekly lesson with joy; it was a bright spot in the monotony of their life. But, after all, this is not so important as it is to teach younger and stronger men and women to earn their living. The needs of the adult blind cannot be covered by an extension of this appropriation or by a development of this kind of teaching. Something new is necessary. Either the scope of the workshop at South Boston must be greatly enlarged, or new ones, independent of it, must be established. It would have been no argument against founding the Massachusetts Institute of Technology to say that there was already a good college across the Charles. He who is content with what has been done is an obstacle in the path of progress.

Up! Up! Something must be done. We have delayed too long. If you want to know how long we have delayed, listen to what the Bishop of Ripon said recently at the Institution for the Blind in Bradford, England. Speaking of a time thirty years ago, he said: "The workhouse and the charity of the passer-by in the street were the only hope of the blind. All that has been changed. The blind have been taught useful occupations, and have been enabled in many cases to earn sufficient to maintain themselves in comfort, so that it has come to be a reproach that a blind man or woman should beg in the streets." This is the change in England in thirty years. There has been no such change in Massachusetts. Something must be done, that is clear. What shall we do?

There are two things to do which work together and become one. First, let the State establish by an adequate appropriation an agency for the employment of the blind. This agency should be in Boston. At the head of it should be a competent man, whose sole duty should be to study all occupations in which the blind can engage, to exhibit the work of the blind, to advise and encourage them, and to bring employers and blind employees together without expense to either* This bureau should do for the blind of Massachusetts what is done by the employment bureau of the British and Foreign Blind Association in England, namely, provide a place in the busiest part of the city, where blind workers and their patrons can be brought together and where articles made by the blind can be advantageously exhibited. The agent should advertise to the public that they can get blind piano tuners, notepaper embossers, shampooers, masseurs, chairmakers, brushmakers, tutors, singers, church organists, tea tasters, and other useful blind people.

Then there is the second part of the work — to increase the variety and efficiency of those other useful blind workers. This means industrial schools; that is, workshops, with all possible machinery and appliances which the blind can profitably handle. To every blind person should be given opportunity to serve an industrial apprenticeship. After he has learned this trade, or that mechanical process, he would go to the agent at the employment bureau, or the agent would go to him, and the agent would then offer to employers the services of a blind workman. In each of the large manufacturing towns — Brockton, Lowell, Taunton, Lawrence, Worcester — there should be a branch of the agency. The head of each branch bureau should know all the industries peculiar to his locality, and should know the employers of the neighbourhood.

Suppose at the age of thirty a man loses his sight, and that means that he must give up his work, let us say, as salesman in a dry goods house. He goes to the nearest agent of the Massachusetts Industrial Bureau for the Blind. The agent knows every occupation in the State which it is profitable for a blind man to engage in, and he tells this man that the best occupation near his home is running a machine of a certain kind. The man then goes to the Industrial School for the Blind and learns to run that machine; in other words he serves an apprenticeship in a free state school, and incidentally learns the other things which a blind man must learn in order to adapt himself to the new conditions of his life; that is, he gets the experience of being blind. At the end of the apprenticeship the agent, knowing what the man can do, goes to a manufacturer and asks that he give the man a chance. The agent stands behind the man during his period of probation, until the employer is convinced that his blind workman understands his business.

Am I dreaming dreams? It is no untried experiment. It is being done in Great Britain. Remember that to educate a blind man so that he becomes a competent workman is no magical and mysterious process. A blind man can do nothing less and nothing more than what a person with five senses can do, minus what can be done only with the eye. Remember, too, that when a man loses his sight he does not know himself what he can do. He needs some one of experience to advise him. The other day the commission listened to a blind man, forty years old, who lost his sight at the age of thirty-six, four years ago. Before he became blind, he had been a lithographer, and was for eight years a foreman. He testified that he was determined not to be a quitter, and that he had tried one and another kind of work, only to fail in each. "What," asked one of the commissioners, "do you think you can learn to do?" "I do not know," replied the man. Do we need a stronger argument for an industrial agency than this answer? Although intelligent and industrious, this man had struggled wildly in the dark for four years, trying in vain to discover what kind of work he had best apply himself to. Think of it! In four years he had had no one to tell him what it was best for him to try to learn to do.

Now who shall change all this? Who shall establish the Massachusetts Industrial Bureau for the Blind? Surely the State — Massachusetts, in whose watchtowers burn continuously the beacons of sympathy and love; Massachusetts, to whom every State in our country turns for example and guidance in education and philanthropy; Massachusetts, in whose beneficent institutions the deaf have learned to speak, the blind to read the printed page, the idiot clay to think. Surely Massachusetts will not now turn a deaf ear to the cry of the helpless adult blind. Has she not lovingly nurtured and abundantly provided for the Perkins Institution and the Kindergarten for the Blind? Once the people learn what should be done, we need not fear that those whose authority is law and those whose authority is loving charity will neglect the sacred duty to raise the adult blind from dependence to self-respecting citizenship. Therefore I have complete faith in the ultimate triumph of our cause.

What the Blind Can Do

The *Youth's Companion,* January 4, 1906.

They meet with darkness in the daytime, and grope at noonday as in the night.
— Job v., 14.

To present to seeing people the truth about the blind is to describe a state of cruel deprivation, and at the same time tell a story of remarkable achievement. It is difficult for those who have not felt the terrors of blindness or known its triumphs to apprehend the position and requirements of the sightless. A great deal has been said and written about the blind; and yet persons well informed on other matters display a mediaeval ignorance about those who cannot see.

I have known intelligent people who believed that the sightless can tell colours by touch, and it is generally thought that they have one or more senses given them in place of the one they have lost, and that the senses which of right belong to them are more delicate and acute than the senses of other people. Nature, herself, we are told, seeks to atone to the blind for their misfortune by giving them a singular sensitiveness and a sweet patience of spirit.

If this were really the case, it would be an advantage rather than an inconvenience to lose one's sight. But it is not the truth; it is a fiction which has its origin in ignorance, and in this ignorance the blind discover the most formidable obstacle in the way to usefulness and independence. Until the public in general better understands the condition of the blind, a condition to which every person is exposed by the vicissitudes of life, it will be impossible to give the blind the special assistance they require. Left without intelligent help, the blind man lives in a night of thwarted instincts and shackled ambitions. Given the right encouragement and aid, he becomes a brave, efficient being, independent himself and of service to others, triumphant over the bondage of darkness.

What is blindness? Close your eyes for a moment. The room you are sitting in, the faces of your loved ones, the books that have been your friends, the games that have delighted you disappear — they all but cease to exist. Go to the window, keeping your eyes shut. God's world — the splendour of sky and sun and moon, almost the charm of human life — has vanished.

Suppose your lids will not open again. What an unspeakable calamity has befallen you! You must begin your life all over in a strange dark world. You must learn to accommodate yourself little by little to the conditions of darkness. You will have to learn the way about your own house. With arms outstretched you must grope from object to object, from room to room?' The tools of your work are snatched from your hands. Your school-books, if you are young, are useless. If you venture out-of-doors, your feet are shod with fear. You are menaced on every side by unseen dangers. The firm earth rolls under your uncertain step. The stars that guided your course are blotted out. You are a human derelict adrift on the world, borne as the currents may chance to set "imprisoned in the viewless winds." In the helplessness of your heart you cry out with the blind man on the plains of Syria, "Thou son of David, have mercy upon me!"

In response to this piteous cry men have stretched forth their hands in sympathy. They could not open the blinded eyes as the Master did on the Syrian plains, but they wrought another miracle — they taught the blind to see with their hands. They could not stay the eclipse of sight, but they pierced the darkness with the light of knowledge. They raised up institutions — temples of compassion — where human skill and science turn affliction and misery to service and happiness.

Since the year 1784, when the Abbé Valentin Hauy gathered together a few blind children from the streets of Paris and began the work of instructing them, the education of the sightless has been continued and extended, until its ever widening embrace of succour and enlightenment has reached the young blind of many countries. Homes and asylums have been provided for the aged and infirm blind. Governments and private philanthropy have united to provide the blind with libraries of embossed books.

Indeed, so much has already been done that I am not surprised to hear you ask, "What good thing yet remains to do for the blind?" I answer, "Help the adult blind to derive all the benefit possible from the education that has been so liberally given them. Help them to become efficient, useful citizens."

When blindness seizes a man in the midst of an active life, he has to face a greater misfortune than the child born blind or deprived of sight in the first years of life. Even if kindness and sympathy surround him, if his family is able to support him and care for him, he nevertheless feels himself a burden.

He finds himself in the state of a helpless child, but with the heart and mind, the desires, instincts, and ambitions of a man. Ignorant of what blind men can do and have done, he looks about him for work, but he looks in vain. Blindness bars every common way to usefulness and independence. Almost every industry, the very machinery of society, the school, the workshop, the factory are all constructed and regulated on the supposition that every one can see.

In the whirl and buzz of a lighted world the blind man, bewildered and helpless, sits down in despair, and resigns himself with bitter patience to a life of inactivity and dependence. It is true that some blind men — men blind from childhood or stricken with blindness in the midst of active lives — have succeeded in almost every known business and profession despite their misfortune. But they have been men of exceptional capacity and energy.

Homer, Ossian, and Milton wrote great poems with never a ray of light in their eyes. Henry Fawcett, professor of political economy at Cambridge University, a member of Parliament for nineteen years, and, during Gladstone's ministry, postmaster-general of Great Britain (he introduced many practical improvements in the postal service, among them the parcels post); Leonhard Euler, the Swiss mathematician and astronomer, who conducted his vast calculations mentally, and who was a member of all the royal societies of learning in Europe; Francois Huber, the naturalist, who was for a century the leading authority on bees; Augustin Thierry, the French historian, who wrote his great work on the Merovingians with the aid of others' eyes; and our own historian, William Hickling Prescott, are blind men who successfully kept in the forefront of life. A distinguished Belgian statesman and writer, Alexander Rodenbach, Didymus of Alexandria, the preceptor of Saint Jerome, Diodotus, the Stoic, friend and teacher of Cicero, Ziska, the leader of the Bohemians in the Hussite War, who thrice defeated the Emperor's forces, did noble work after their eyes had ceased to know the light. Blind men have been musicians, road-builders, carpenters, wood-workers, journalists, editors, yacht-builders, and teachers of the blind and the seeing.

These indomitable blind men wrought out their own salvation, and became the liberators of their afflicted fellows by proving what man can do in the dark by the light of courage and intelligence. For it must be seen that if an exceptional blind man, unaided by a special education in a school for the blind, can lead a life of service and distinction, an ordinary blind man without genius can be trained to do an ordinary man's work; and this tells us what yet remains to do for the blind.

American commonwealths and philanthropists have always been generous to the blind. The states have provided excellent schools, generally based on sound and beneficent principles, for their blind children and youths. In many of these institutions the standard is high, and the pupils attain marked proficiency in all the common school branches. But for all the munificence of individual charity and the liberality of public endowment, the blind man is still lost to the community as a producer. Education, books, science, music do not make the blind happy unless they enable them to work. Philanthropy which only rears fine buildings equipped with the implements of learning, and does not render its beneficiaries stronger and more serviceable citizens, annuls by unwisdom the generosity that inspires it, and makes void its charity.

Blind graduates of these schools have said to me, in the bitterness of disappointed hopes and ambitions, "It would have been better to leave us in ignorance than to enlighten and cultivate our minds only to plunge us into a double darkness. What boots it that we have spent our youth in kindergartens, museums, libraries, and music-rooms if we pass from those pleasant halls to sit with idle hands and eat the dry crust of discontent?" The time has come when strong and efficient measures should be taken in America to give the blind an opportunity to become self-supporting, or at least to earn a part of their support. In an age when the ability to work is regarded almost as a test of respectability, it is a disgrace that any man should be forced to sit in idleness.

The blind as a rule are poor. The parents of most of the children in the institutions for the blind are working people, and the man struck blind by accident or disease is usually a bread-winner. It is not uncommon for a young man to lose his sight in such occupations as stone-cutting, diamond-polishing, glazing, and blasting rocks. Without assistance, men thus blinded are doomed to involuntary idleness for the rest of their lives.

Up to the present day no adequate provision has been made for this class of blind persons in America, although Dr. Samuel G. Howe, the friend of all the afflicted and the pioneer in the education of the blind in the United States, outlined a plan to meet the industrial requirements of the adult blind more than sixty years ago. No other American has understood the sightless so thoroughly as Doctor Howe. He knew their weakness and how they might be strengthened. All his efforts in their behalf and all that he wrote about them show his discerning love and wisdom. He was one of the first to realize that there is something better even than feeding the hungry and clothing the naked, that it is a greater kindness to help them feed and clothe themselves. I do not know how I can better indicate the way in which the blind should be helped than by giving a summary of Doctor Howe's conclusions.

"If every child born into the community," says Doctor Howe, "has a right to food for his body and knowledge for his mind, then has he a right to some useful employment, for without it food and knowledge become but curses; they had better have been withheld."

Upon this broad and humane principle he organized the Perkins Institution for the Blind in Boston. Its first object was to instruct and enlighten the young blind, its second to enable the blind to earn their own livelihood. Accordingly, in 1840, he established a work department where those who had finished their education could pursue for their own profit the trades they had learned in school.

His annual reports furnish an interesting account of the ups and downs of his experiment. When a new enterprise is undertaken, it often happens that obstacles and difficulties are disregarded which later compel us to pause and consider. In the first enthusiasm of his work in behalf of the blind, Doctor Howe confidently expected that the great majority of the blind would be able to support themselves by means of their brains — they would be musicians, teachers, journalists, and ministers of the gospel. The less gifted blind could earn their living by manual labour, with a little assistance and direction from their alma mater.

These expectations were doomed to disappointment. Not all blind persons are highly gifted. They do not all possess musical talent or extraordinary intellectual capacity; nor do they all have the energy and perseverance necessary to overcome the heavy handicap that they encounter at the start. If all the blind were Miltons and Rodenbachs, they would need no such champion as Doctor Howe — no Moses would be necessary if there were no wilderness.

But although disappointed and often discouraged, Doctor Howe did not lose heart. Experience taught him the real wants of the blind and the best way to meet them. The failure of his high expectations showed him the imperative necessity of training the blind for some useful if less ambitious occupation. He urged that the institutions should supplement their instruction by aiding their graduates in their attempts to become self-supporting.

The institutions, that is, should be the capitalists of the blind, but should seek no pecuniary advantage for themselves. They should be willing to make a considerable outlay in the beginning, and indeed to the end, if necessary. Their object should be to aid the blind to counteract the disadvantages under which they work by bringing them as near as possible to an equality of opportunity with other workmen.

Such were Doctor Howe's views when he opened a workshop for blind adults under the auspices of the Perkins Institution. The aim of the workshop was to give the blind the advantages which seeing workmen have — of working in a company, of saving rent and fuel and other incidental expenses, of having capital, and obtaining their stock at wholesale cost, and getting their produce cheaply marketed. The shop, said Doctor Howe, should train them in diligence and skill; then if the world did not offer a field for the exercise of their talents, the institution should try to open one for them.

At the end of five years we find Doctor Howe optimistic about his experiment, and full of plans to extend the work so as to include a salesroom in the city for the reception and sale of articles made by the blind at home. Indeed, he looked forward to the foundation of an establishment broad enough to meet the wants of all the blind of New England. Would such an establishment, providing for so many persons, support itself? he asked. The answer was uncertain; but he argued that even if very few of the blind succeeded in becoming fully self-supporting, it was still good economy to enable them to earn as much of their support as possible. The State should help them indirectly in this way rather than pay their board and lodging. But, after all, the first consideration of a wise commonwealth is not economy, but the good of all its citizens.

We must cross the Atlantic and visit the Old World in order to find a practical demonstration of what the blind can do. The first institution for the employment of the blind was founded at Edinburgh in 1793. Since then workshops, salesrooms, and associations or agencies to promote the business interests of the blind have been established in Europe.

In Europe the emphasis has been upon industrial training, while in America more attention has been given to book education. When a pupil in a school for the blind in England or France shows no special aptitude for music or intellectual pursuits, he is put into the work department, where he learns a trade. Afterward the institution, or one of the agencies for the purpose in his country, seeks out a position for him, and stands by him until he has proved his efficiency. On the other hand, when a student shows marked ability in any direction, he receives opportunity to fit himself for a more responsible position. If a school for the blind has trained an organist who is capable of filling a church position, the agencies for the blind keep a lookout for a vacancy.

When the agent hears of one, he goes to the place and tells the church committee of a blind man who is competent to fill the position. The committee is probably very skeptical and very reluctant to try so doubtful an experiment. The agent, however, is eloquent, and persuades the committee to give the man a trial. The man comes, plays, and conquers.

In London there is a tea agency of which the managers are wholly or partially blind. Many blind agents are selling its teas, coffees, and cocoas in all parts of England.

Last June there was held in Edinburgh an exhibition of the work of the blind all over the world. A whole floor was devoted to weaving machines and typewriters, and blind people demonstrated their skill as weavers, masseurs, carpenters, and musicians. At the Glasgow Asylum the blind have produced salable articles for eighty years, and in three recent years the average annual sales amounted to twenty-nine thousand pounds sterling.

In English cities from 6 to 13 per cent, of the blind are in workshops, while in America, of sixty-four thousand blind persons only six hundred, or 1 per cent., are employed in industrial establishments.

But a brighter day dawned for the blind in America when New York and Massachusetts awoke to the necessity of looking into the condition of the sightless. Connecticut, Pennsylvania, Wisconsin, California, and Michigan are all active in the effort to make wage-earners of the blind. The nature of the work which has begun, and should be extended as rapidly as possible, is represented by the endeavours of the Massachusetts Association to Promote the Interests of the Adult Blind.

This association has opened an experiment station in Cambridge, to find and test industries that seem practicable for the sightless. The blind are sought out in their homes, and when possible they are taught trades, their work is brought to the notice of the public, and the capacity of blind men and women to operate certain automatic machines in factories is demonstrated to employers.

Hitherto the chief industries of the blind have been the manufacture of brooms, mattresses, baskets, brushes, and mats, not all of which are profitable in this country. The effort should be to increase the number of possible lucrative occupations for the sightless.

A young blind man was trained at the station in Cambridge in ten days to cut box corners in a paper and tag factory to the satisfaction of his employer. Another young man has succeeded in taking, by means of a shorthand writing machine, acceptable interviews for a newspaper. A young blind woman was taken from the poorhouse, where she had been for three years, and placed in a hairpin factory, where she has found work that she is capable of doing.

The experiment station is now at work on a patented mop invented by a blind man. This "Wonder mop" can be made entirely without sight, and the plan is to have blind agents from Maine to California sell it. If the mop proves as successful as it now promises to be, it will go a long way toward solving the industrial problem of the blind in this country.

What the blind workman needs is an industry that will enable him to produce something that people will buy, not out of pity for him, but because it is useful or beautiful. The blind will not lack for customers if their articles are of the best material, design, and workmanship.

The little group of workers at the experiment station have received more orders for their beautiful rugs, sofa pillows, and table covers than their limited means and inadequate space enable them to fill promptly. Workers for the blind have found both manufacturers and employers ready and glad to cooperate with them when they understand that it is opportunity and not charity that is asked.

There is no law on the statute-books compelling people to move up closer on the bench of life to make room for a blind brother; but there is a divine law written on the hearts of men constraining them to make a place for him, not only because he is unfortunate, but also because it is his right as a human being to share God's greatest gift, the privilege of man to go forth unto his work.

Preventable Blindness

The *Ladies' Home Journal,* January, 1907.

We all know that a large number of people become blind every year. But it is not generally known that many human eyes are needlessly lost which, if right corrective and preventive measures were employed, would be saved to the service of the world. And what we should know, in particular, is that much of this blindness can be prevented by the mothers themselves.

We live in an epoch of reform. I read that men and women are valiantly contending against the greed and neglect that condemn thousands of children to dwarf their minds and bodies in labour; I hear that we are striving to protect ourselves against impure food and dangerous "patent medicines." But of all ignorance which needs to be dispelled by the spirit of regeneration among us, none is more intolerable than that which wantonly permits children to be plunged into the abyss of blindness.

Two fifths of all blindness could have been prevented by precautionary or curative treatment. Of this, one quarter, or one tenth of the whole, is due to what is called "ophthalmia neonatorum" — that is, "infantile ophthalmia."

"What is ophthalmia neonatorum?" It is an inflammation of the eyes which attacks the new-born child and is one of the most prolific causes of blindness. It is occasioned by germs finding an entrance in the eyes of the child during the process of birth. In from twenty-four to sixty hours after the birth of the child whose eyes have been infected the eyes grow red and a watery secretion comes from the lids. This soon grows thicker and more profuse until a creamy discharge pours out from the eyes. The lids become swollen, hard and red. If this condition is allowed to continue, the eyeballs become ulcerated until finally they rupture and the child in many cases becomes blind.

All this can be prevented. If, at the time of birth, the baby's eyelids are gently wiped dry with a little absorbent cotton and the lids held open while the eyes are flushed with a saline solution — as warm and as salt as normal tears — the malignant germs *may* be washed away and the danger averted.

But as it is not always possible for those with untrained hands to accomplish this skilfully and thoroughly, and as under any circumstances we cannot be certain that all of the virulent microscopic germs are removed, it is necessary as a further step that one or two drops of a solution of nitrate of silver of a determined strength be dropped in each eye of the new-born child. Should a strong solution be used, as it may be by the physician, it should be immediately neutralized by a few drops of slightly salted boiled water; with a weaker solution this neutralization is not necessary. This silver preparation destroys the germs without injuring the eyes and its use practically eliminates this frightful disease as a cause of blindness.

As it is never possible to know in which baby's eyes the germs have found lodgment, and as the use of the silver is safe and sure, the preventive solution should be invariably employed at every birth. To delay or omit it is to invite unnecessary danger.

It happens, however, in a few cases, even where silver nitrate is used, that some of the microbes escape destruction and remain to threaten the sight. This does not mean that all is lost, that the child's chances are gone. The same remedy judiciously applied at a sufficiently early period in the progress of the disease and under competent medical advice will destroy the germs and thereby control the inflammation and still prevent blindness.

Since the value and importance of this measure is universally conceded, and its employment commended by the medical profession, it would seem remarkable that it does not form a part of the toilet of every newborn child, and the inquiry is naturally suggested: why is it not always employed in the eyes of the new-born? How can it ever happen that so simple a preventive measure can be omitted, when its neglect leads to such disastrous consequences? In almost all the large hospitals and in the practice of nearly every careful scientific physician it is, indeed, a routine measure, but ignorance, indifference, and negligence are still abroad in the land, and until those shall be aroused who feel a moral responsibility in defending the rights of the helpless infant thus cruelly assailed, babies will be blinded and lives will be blighted, world without end.

There would seem to be three reasons why every physician (and every midwife who takes the physician's responsibilities at a birth) does not invariably employ a silver solution in the eyes of every new-born child: first, many who have to deal with the expectant mother are not acquainted with the character of this germ disease and have not yet learned the importance and necessity of preventive measures; others hesitate to employ this valuable specific from a wrong impression that it may harm the tender eye of the infant child; but the neglect in far the greater number of cases is due to the fact that the silver solution does not happen to be present at the moment at which it is needed, and as the majority of children escape infection, the chance is taken that each child may be one of the fortunate. The propitious moment at which the silver nitrate might be effectively employed is allowed to pass, and when next the opportunity comes it may be too late.

In order that this pitiable condition be not allowed to continue, two things should be done at once. A campaign of education should be inaugurated and every expectant mother should be made acquainted with the peril which may threaten her child so that she may insist that it be protected; and then the State should freely and gratuitously place in the hands of every accoucheur an aseptic silver solution that carries with it the assurance on the part of the highest medical authority as to its necessity, its purity, and its safety.

There is but one reason why this great movement should not quickly and effectively succeed in abolishing infantile ophthalmia as a cause of blindness, and that is — general apathy. In order that the necessary and uniform legislation be secured in every State, efforts must be made. The mothers in every State must demand it. In every class of society the women should know of the cause and dangers of this disease.

If the mothers of America could be made to realize that their babies are in danger of losing their sight, and that the dread calamity can be warded off by applying a simple, precautionary remedy at the right time, they would be quick to demand of those in authority that the symptoms of the disease shall be known by those whose duty it is to know them, and that for safety the remedy shall be at hand before the symptoms appear.

A careful examination of the children of the New York School for the Blind for several years showed that among city children ophthalmia neonatorum causes one case of blindness in three. In the country the relative number of cases resulting from infantile ophthalmia is greater than in the cities. The reason for this is that, though the disease is widespread, a physician in a small community may never have seen a case. He may not recognize the disease if it appears. If he knows about the nitrate of silver treatment he may fail to use it because he wrongly fears that it may injure the delicate eyes of the child. He may not see the child again for several days; then the disease has got beyond his control. The cornea is destroyed and the infant's sight irrecoverably lost! The safe rule for physicians is to regard with suspicion the slightest inflammation in the eyes of an infant, and it is the rule for mothers, too; for the mother who is watchful and informed will know how to make the right demand upon her physician.

The mother thinks with joy and pride that her child will grow in God's light to be a strong man, able to do a man's work. Suddenly she is plunged into the crudest anguish by the discovery that her child's beautiful eyes are put out forever. Not till then does she realize how terrible is the foe that has lurked by his cradle. Imagine her feelings if afterward she learns that this disaster was needless, that it could have been avoided by prompt, efficient measures. Her grief is embittered by indignation against the physician in whose hand she had placed the safety of her child. Whatever may be done to soften the misfortune of the child, her heart will never be whole again.

Blindness in infancy is worse in some ways than blindness in late childhood, or even in adult life. It arrests development. The plight of the blind baby is indeed heartrending. He loses much of the physical activity and incentive and the various intellectual experiences of the normal child. Even in the best of homes it is not often possible to give him the special, constant care, teaching and encouragement that he requires. He is not admitted to the kindergarten for the blind, if there be one, until he is five years old. In the meantime he grows weak and deformed in body and mind, and acquires nervous habits which it is extremely hard to break when his education begins. Your heart aches as you look at him, feeble, pitiful, enervated, beside his strong, merry comrades who have lost their sight at a later period, and who can go forward with firm steps where he halts and stumbles. Even if he is successfully taught, and develops capabilities, even if he is not doomed in his mature years, as are so many of the blind, to idleness and dependence, his loss of sight is irreparable. A blind person, however well instructed, however carefully equipped, can never be so free, so self-reliant as if he had his eyes. In this country, until very recently, little has been done to enable the grown-up blind to work for a livelihood, to earn their limited share of independence and self-support. They are for the most part poor, and if no relative or friend cares for them they become objects of charity, a burden to the State. Such is the lot of thousands of men and women who a generation ago needlessly lost their sight. Such is the fate that threatens our little ones to-day.

It is true that we are preparing to take better and better care of the blind. Intelligent work is going forward all over the country to lighten the burden of blindness. But, however merry our blind children, however brave and self-reliant our blind men, I say, could the utmost dreams of education for the sightless be realized, the dark is still the dark, and blindness an irremediable calamity.

Therefore I say, let us check this dread disease and danger. The State should require that every case of disease of the eye in the newborn be reported. If blindness follows, then an investigation should be instituted. The certainty that such an investigation would surely follow would compel physician and nurse to exercise the utmost care in the treatment of the new-born.

By such vigilance on the part of the Commonwealth hundreds of individuals would be spared misery and dependence, and the Commonwealth itself would be saved expense. The entire cost of preventing ophthalmia is indeed an ounce of prevention to the many pounds that avoidable blindness costs the State. The cost of educating a blind child in a good school is three hundred dollars a year. The special expense necessary to make a blind man self-supporting, even in conditions far better than now exist, must be an extra expense to the State. If, as is the too common case, a blind citizen becomes dependent through a long life, the average sum spent for his maintenance is ten thousand dollars. This sum must be multiplied many times to determine the total loss; for by blindness a productive breadwinner is removed from the community.

If a tithe of the money we now spend to support unnecessary blindness were spent to prevent it, the State would be the gainer in terms of cold economy, not to speak of considerations of happiness and humanity. How, then, can a wise Commonwealth suffer a single case of avoidable blindness to pass unquestioned? We pay money in advance to insure our property and the property value of our lives. Yet we have not the foresight to insure our children against the bitter and costly evil of blindness!

In ancient times disease was looked upon as a curse to be conjured away. Later it was regarded as a necessary misfortune to be cured or alleviated. In our own time it is known to be the result of wrong living, and therefore to be avoided and prevented. Prevention has come to be the all-important aim of medical science. The fight to exterminate yellow fever and tuberculosis is a greater battle than any that the doctors have waged against disease after it has seized upon the patient. If our physicians have undertaken to exterminate so subtle an enemy as tuberculosis, they should make short work of ophthalmia neonatorum, which is obvious and easily cured. To do battle with it our physicians must march as soldiers have gone forth before, ordered by the State and urged on by women. American women can accomplish almost anything that they set their hearts on, and the mothers of the land together with the physicians can abolish infantile ophthalmia, yes, wipe it out of the civilized world.

The Plain Truth

Address at the annual convention of the American Association of Workers for the Blind, Boston, August 27, 1907.

In behalf of the Massachusetts Commission for the Blind I welcome to Boston this association of workers for the sightless. The purpose of our convention which represents every movement to better the condition of the blind, is to secure cooperation between the institutions and societies which are concerned in our problem. I know that good will come of our taking counsel together. I feel that we have the fair-mindedness to look at facts squarely, and the courage to set out hopefully, on the long road which stretches before us.

Our problem is complicated, and has more sides than isolated effort, however zealous, can compass. We must see to it that in the diversity of interests one class of the blind is not overlooked for the sake of another, or any part of the work undervalued.

The workshop, the library of embossed books, the home for the aged blind, the nursery, the kindergarten and the school are seen to be parts of a system with one end in view. I rejoice that there is assembled here a company of men and women determined to take to heart all the needs of all the blind, and in the name of the blind and of the State whose commission I represent I bid you welcome.

We have been forced to realize the shortcomings of our system, or lack of system, wherein faithful workers go in opposite directions, each hugging a private book of embossed type, or the plans of an institution which is to be the best and only seat of salvation for the blind. Let us draw our forces together. However we differ in the details of our work, let us unite in the conviction that the essential thing is to give the blind something they can do with brain and hand. The higher education, in which some of us are particularly interested, depends largely on early training in childhood, on healthy surroundings at school, on physical happiness, play, and out-of-door exercise.

Besides the young blind, for whom existing institutions are intended to provide, there is the numerous class of active, useful men and women who lose their sight in mature years. Those who are in the dark from childhood are hard pressed by obstacles. But the man suddenly stricken blind is another Samson, bound captive, helpless until we unloose his chains.

This association may become an organized power which will carry knowledge of the needs of the blind to every corner of the country. It may bring about cooperation, and good-will between schools, associations and all sincere workers for the sightless. It may start or stimulate efficient work in States which are yet in original darkness. Blindness must always remain an evil, whatever we do to make it bearable. We must strike at the root of blindness and labour to diminish and prevent it.

The problem of prevention should be dealt with frankly.

Physicians, as we are glad to see they are doing, shall take pains to disseminate knowledge needful for a clear understanding of the causes of blindness.

The time for hinting at unpleasant truths is past. Let us insist that the States put into practice every known and approved method of prevention, and that physicians and teachers open the doors of knowledge wide for the people to enter in. The facts are not agreeable reading, often they are revolting. But it is better that our sensibilities should be shocked than that we should be ignorant of facts upon which rest sight, hearing, intelligence, morals and the life of the children of men.

Let us do our best to rend the thick curtain with which society is hiding its eyes from unpleasant but needful truth. No organization is doing its duty that only bestows charity and does not also communicate the knowledge which saves and blesses.

We read that in one year Indiana has appropriated over a million dollars to aid and increase institutions for the blind, the deaf, the insane, the feeble-minded, the epileptical. Surely the time has come for us to ask plain questions and to receive plain answers. While we do our part to alleviate present disease, let us press forward in the scientific study which shall reveal our bodies as sacred temples of the soul.

When the promises of the future are fulfilled and we rightly understand our bodies and our responsibilities toward unborn generations, the institutions for defectives which are now our pride will become terrible monuments to our ignorance and the needless misery that we once endured.

The Truth Again

The *Ladies' Home Journal,* January, 1909.

A year ago I wrote about the prevention of blindness, I wrote guardedly and with hesitation; for the subject was new to me, and I shrank from discussing before the general public a problem which hitherto had been confined to conferences of specialists. Moreover, the subject was one of which a young yeoman might be supposed to be ignorant, and upon which, certainly, she would not be expected to speak with authority. It is always painful to set one's self against tradition, especially against the conventions and prejudices that hedge about womanhood. But continuous study of blindness has forced upon me knowledge of this subject, and, if I am to stand as an advocate of the work for the sightless, I cannot, without accusing myself of cowardice, gloss over or ignore the fundamental evil.

Once I believed that blindness, deafness, tuberculosis and other causes of suffering were necessary, unpreventable. I believed that we must accept blind eyes, deaf ears, diseased lungs as we accept the havoc of tornadoes and deluges, and that we must bear them with as much fortitude as we could gather from religion and philosophy. But gradually my reading extended, and I found that those evils are to be laid not at the door of Providence, but at the door of mankind; that they are, in large measure, due to ignorance, stupidity, and sin.

The most common cause of blindness is ophthalmia of the new-born. One pupil in every three at the institution for the blind in New York City was blinded in infancy by this disease. Nearly all of the sixteen babies in the Sunshine Home in Brooklyn, one fourth of the inmates of the New York State Home for the Blind, six hundred sightless persons in the State of New York, between six thousand and seven thousand persons in the United States, were plunged into darkness by ophthalmia of the new-born. The symptoms of the disease appear in the infant's eyes soon after birth. The eyelids swell and become red, and about the second day they discharge whitish pus. At this stage the eyes can be saved by the simplest prophylactic care. That such care is not always exercised is due to the fact that one half of the cases of childbirth in America are attended by midwives many of whom are ignorant and incompetent. In this country very little has been done to secure the proper education and examination of midwives; and they and the equally ignorant parents resort to poultices, nostrums, and domestic remedies.

There is a remedy for ophthalmia neonatorum. This is an instillation of nitrate of silver solution into the eyes of the child. It is efficacious if promptly and skilfully applied. It is not, however, infallible, and in unskilful hands it may do great harm. The mother who sees in the eyes of her baby the symptoms which I have described should lose no time in summoning the assistance of an intelligent physician.

Let no one suppose that this is idle advice. In France and Germany the laws require that the eyes of every child shall be treated with nitrate of silver solution as soon as it is born, and in those countries there has been a considerable decrease in blindness resulting from the scourge of ophthalmia neonatorum. And what do the wise lawmakers of America do? A bill for the prevention of blindness introduced recently in the Illinois Legislature failed to pass because it was argued that this was only another scheme of doctors to provide fees for themselves! But, at best, the law is concerned only with the remedy. The people themselves, and only they, can wipe out the cause.

What is the cause of ophthalmia neonatorum? It is a specific germ communicated by the mother to the child at birth. Previous to the child's birth she has unconsciously received it through infection from her husband. He has contracted the infection in licentious relations before or since marriage. "The crudest link in the chain of consequences," says Dr. Prince Morrow, "is the mother's innocent agency. She is made a passive, unconscious medium of instilling into the eyes of her new-born babe a virulent poison which extinguishes its sight."

In mercy let it be remembered, the father does not know that he has so foully destroyed the eyes of his child and handicapped him for life. It is part of the bitter harvest of the wild oats he has sown. Society has smiled upon his "youthful recklessness" because Society does not know that

"They enslave their children's children who make compromise with sin."

Society has yet to learn that the blind beggar at the street-corner, the epileptic child, the woman on the operating-table, are the wages of "youthful indiscretion." To-day science is verifying what the Old Testament taught three thousand years ago, and the time has come when there is no longer the excuse of ignorance. Knowledge has been given us; it is our part to apply it.

Of the consequences of social sin, blindness is by no means the most terrible. The same infection which blots out the eyes of the baby is responsible for many childless homes; for thousands of cases of lifelong invalidism; for 80 per cent, of all inflammatory diseases peculiar to women; and for 75 per cent, of all operations performed on mothers to save their lives.

The day has come when women must face the truth. They cannot escape the consequences of the evil unless they have the knowledge that saves. Must we leave young girls to meet the danger in the dark because we dare not turn the light upon our social wickedness? False delicacy and prudery must give place to precise information and common sense. It is high time to abolish falsehood and let the plain truth come in. Out with the cowardice which shuts its eyes to the immorality that causes disease and human misery! I am confident that when the people know the truth the day of deliverance for mother and child will be at hand.

We must look to it that every child is protected before his birth. Every child has a right to be well born. Every child has a right to be told by his parents and teachers about his birth and his body; for in such knowledge lie true innocence and safety. Civilization is menaced by an insidious enemy. It must learn that only one cure is sure and cheap: right living, which God gives free to all. And right living depends on right knowledge.

We must set to work in the right direction the three great agencies which inform and educate us: the church, the school, and the press. If they remain silent, obdurate, they will bear the odium which recoils upon evildoers. They may not listen at first to our plea for light and knowledge. They may combine to baffle us; but there will rise, again and again, to confront them, the beseeching forms of little children: deaf, blind, crooked of limb, and vacant of mind.

This is not faultfinding. I am not a pessimist, but an optimist, by temperament and conviction. I am making a plea for American women and their children. I plead that the blind may see, the deaf may hear, and the idiot may have a mind. In a word, I plead that the American woman may be the mother of a great race.

Throw aside, I beseech you, false modesty — the shame that shelters evil — and hasten the day when there shall be no preventable disease among mankind.

The Conservation of Eyesight

Address at a meeting of The Massachusetts Association for Promoting the Interests of the Blind, Boston, February 14, 1911.

I rejoice that the greatest of all work for the blind — the saving of eyesight — has been so clearly laid before the public. The reports of progress in the conservation of eyes, of health, of life, and of all things precious to man, are as a trumpet blast summoning us to still greater effort. The devotion of physicians and laymen and the terrible needs of our fellow-men ought to hearten us in the fight against conquerable misery.

Our worst foes are ignorance, poverty, and the unconscious cruelty of our commercial society. These are the causes of blindness; these are the enemies which destroy the sight of children and workmen and undermine the health of mankind. So long as these enemies remain unvanquished, so long will there be blind and crippled men and women.

To study the diseases and accidents which cause loss of sight, and to learn how the surgeon can prevent or alleviate them, is not enough. We should strive to put an end to the conditions which produce the diseases and accidents.

This case of blindness, the physician says, resulted from ophthalmia. It was really caused by a dark, overcrowded room, by the indecent herding together of human beings in unsanitary tenements. We are told that another case of blindness resulted from the bursting of a wheel. The true cause was an employer's failure to safeguard his machine. Investigations show that there are many ingenious safeguards for machinery which are not adopted because their adoption would diminish the manufacturer's profits. We Americans have been slow, dishonourably slow, in taking measures for the protection of our workmen.

Does it occur to any of you that the white lace which we wear is darkened by the failing eyes of the maker? The trouble is that most of us do not understand the essential relation between poverty and disease. I do not believe that there is any one in this City of Kind Hearts who would willingly receive dividends if he knew that they had been paid in part with blinded eyes and broken backs. If you doubt that there is any such connection between our prosperity and the sorrows of others, consult those bare but illuminating reports of industrial commissions and labour bureaus. They are less eloquent than oratory, less pleasant than fiction, but more convincing than either. In them you will find the fundamental causes of much blindness and crookedness, of shrunken limbs and degraded minds. These causes must be further searched out, and every condition in which blindness breeds must be exposed and abolished. Let our battle cry be, "No preventable disease, no unnecessary poverty, no blinding ignorance among mankind."

The Training of a Blind Child

The *Ladies' Home Journal,* April, 1908.

For many centuries after the coming of Christ, blindness, deafness, and mental defects were regarded as the visitations of Providence, to be borne with meekness and fortitude. This old misreading of the message of Christianity still persists in some unhappy minds. There are mothers who object to having an afflicted child taught, lest the more he knows the less resigned he will be to a divine decree. Recently a case came to my knowledge of a devoted parent who kept a deaf girl out of school in order that she might not lose "her beautiful spirit of resignation." The truer Christianity teaches us that disease and ignorance are not ultimate decrees of Heaven, and that such discontent as the first visions of light bring to the yearning soul is a divine discontent. The finest resignation and submission are not incompatible with heroic contest against the forces of darkness. The old idea was to endure. This was succeeded by a better idea, to alleviate and cure. And that, in turn, has given way to the modern idea, to prevent, to root out diseases that destroy the sight, the hearing, the mind, the life and the morals of men. Physicians like Pasteur and Koch, soldiers like Major Walter Reed, and other men of the American Army who gave their lives in a grim war of extermination against disease — these are the leaders of a new cohort of crusaders who are fighting the true battle of God against the infidel. We know now that hospitals and institutions for defectives are not permanent temples of salvation. They are, rather, like temporary camp-sites along the way upon which the race is journeying toward a city where disease and darkness shall not be.

I have already written about the prevention of unnecessary blindness. We know that much of it can be prevented by simple timely measures. But so long as the laws of health and right living are violated, any mother may have the anguish of seeing her child's beautiful eyes closed to the light forever. Hence, all mothers, nurses, and teachers should have some knowledge of the methods of training blind children. On the American mother the schools for the blind — and for the seeing — depend for support, encouragement, intelligent criticism. Moreover, the work of the schools is helped or thwarted by the care which the children receive before they are old enough to go school.

There are in this country thousands of blind children under school age. Many of them are growing up helpless, untrained, and suffering from want of exercise and play. In order to understand their needs let us imagine what happens when a child loses his sight. He is suddenly shut out from all familiar things, from his games, his studies and the society of other children. The experience and incentive to action that come to us largely through the eye are arrested. The toys that ere while charmed him with bright colours fall meaningless from his little hands. The picture of tree or bird that he drew in the flush of delight in a newly acquired art is a blank to him. He runs no more to gaze at the changing scenes of the city street or at the sights of the country that fly thick as driving rain. He has lost a world of stimuli, the free motion and the restless out-reachings of sense which animate us from the earliest years. He ceases to imitate, because he sees nothing to imitate, and imitation is essential to growth. He no longer plays the king, the soldier, the sailor, the giant.

He was but a recipient of life from life of impulses that pushed him to action. He listened to life, he saw it gleam, and every instinct within him felt a stir of might, and, grasping at the clews of sense, embodied itself in his act, his look, his word. This was the natural way of beginning his existence. In those glimpses, those bursts of sound, he grew. They are now withdrawn, and the activity which flooded his being has ebbed away. Small, tottering, bewildered, he must begin life again. A new sense must be developed that shall bring back the stimuli and set aglow again the joy of his heart. The new sense is touch. He must learn to use his hands instead of his eyes. Flung upon a wholly strange world, he must learn to play again, but in the dark; he must grow in the dark, work in the dark, and perhaps die in the dark. We are ready to understand now what must be supplied to him and to the child blind at infancy.

The devices for teaching and amusing a sightless child at home are simple and within the reach of intelligent parents. A blind child should have plenty of objects that he can feel, throw around, hunt for, put in his mouth, if he likes. He will learn their qualities. Touchable qualities are countless; round, flat, smooth, rough, soft and hard, cold and hot, sharp, pointed and blunt, fat, thin, silky, velvety. The elements of beauty, order, form, symmetry, are within his reach. Try to refine his touch, so that he may delight in feeling graceful lines, curves, and motions, and you will thereby refine his mind and tastes.

Encourage him to examine the properties of everything that he can safely touch. He should not, however, be allowed to remain a sedentary investigator, using only the small muscles of his fingers. The wider the range of his explorations the stouter and braver the young navigator will grow. He can go sailing on the wide, wide ocean if he piles up chairs for a ship and hoists a cloth for a sail. A rocking-chair makes a fine locomotive, wherewith to cross continents, but the young engineer should not sit in it; he should push it from behind, that his legs may grow sturdy. Without strength gained from vigorous action he will profit little by the knowledge gained from more delicate activities. There is time enough for these when his legs are weary and he is ready to sit down. Then he can find multifold exercise for his flexible, inquisitive fingers. He can weave tape in and out through the back rods of a chair, cut paper (with blunt-pointed scissors), make chains of spools, beads or daisies. Let him model with clay or putty, put together sliced maps and puzzles. Such play exercises his ingenuity, brings firmness and precision of touch, fosters observation. Teach him to spin tops, for he will find neverending pleasure in their whirl and hum. I used to love to spin dollars and every other thing that would spin. I remember a set of stone blocks with which I joyed to build cathedrals, castles, houses, bridges. Finally I asked for a toy city, entire, including churches with steeples, a schoolhouse, a hospital, a square full of trees and houses with steep roofs and plenty of doors and windows. Sometimes I flung all the buildings down, pretending it was an earthquake. Then I dropped apples in the midst of the town and cried, "Vesuvius has erupted!"

The toy-shops, with their wonderful mechanical playthings, their ingenious miniatures of all the furniture of life, will supply apparatus enough for the blind child's home school, and, even if the teacher-mother cannot afford to buy toys, she will find suggestions for homemade ones.

But the toy is merely an adjunct. Child and mother can turn the commonest things, indoors and out, into the materials of play. The all-important object is interesting exercise. Do not let your blind child lie on the bed in the daytime or rest in the corner "out of harm's way." Pull the mattress into the middle of the room, and teach him to turn somersaults on it. Let him cling to your dress or your arm as you go about your work. Even if it inconveniences you, it will teach him to walk steadily and to find his way about the house. Encourage him to run, skip, jump, fly in the swing, and give his playmates a push when they take their turn at swinging. Children are sympathetic and quick to learn. They will lead their blind comrade into their games, especially if they receive the right suggestions from the parents. When the blind child wrestles and plays rough-and-tumble with the other children the unwise mother will run to rescue the afflicted contestant; the wise mother will applaud the struggle so long as it is sportsmanlike and good-natured.

When it is possible, the blind child should be taught to swim and to row. If there is a yard or garden with definite boundaries let him be familiar with every part of it. Furnish him with a sandpile, spade, and shovel; show him how to plant, pick flowers, and water them. Before my teacher came to me I used to hang to my mother's skirt or to my nurse, and I picked strawberries, watered the flowers, turned the ice-cream freezer, folded clothes, and helped the cook pluck the fowl — much to the cook's annoyance. This was an ignorant activity on my part, for I had no language, and therefore no knowledge. How much more is open to the blind child who has learned the language of affection and can be stimulated by the thought that he is "helping mother!" This will develop a love of usefulness, the inspiring sense that he is of service to his family.

It is needful that the mother be ever ready with a suggestion of something new, for the child will tire of doing one thing long. If he is in the country he can feed the poultry, the dog and the cat, shell peas, string beans, peel apples, set the table, wipe dishes, dust, put things in place, and some of these activities are possible in the city, too. That day has been well spent which leaves the blind child in state of healthy fatigue ready to go to sleep. A great many blind persons have insomnia due to nervousness and lack of exercise. Indeed

— and mark this well — it is not blindness, but the afflictions that accompany it and result from it, that make the blind miserable and inefficient.

The mother who knows that she has it in her power to restore to her blind child almost everything but the mere act of seeing will find in his deprivation, not a calamity to cast her down, but an opportunity to develop her tact, patience, wisdom — an object on which to bestow the highest gifts that have been vouchsafed to her.

Laugh and talk with your blind child as you look and smile at your seeing child. Pass his hand lightly over your features and let him feel, not for long, but attentively, the play of facial expression. The face speaks eloquently by unconscious movements of the muscles, as in the smile, the set grave look, the quiver of the lips. Tears, the hot flush of the cheek, the toss of the head, the look downward or upward, are the true indices of mood and emotion. The child will learn these expressions, come in time to imitate them, and thus show an animated face. It is very necessary for the blind child to have a face which speaks to the world of seeing persons in the language which they are accustomed to read in each other's countenances. Without that he will be isolated and misunderstood. People shrink from a blind-looking face and mistake its blankness for want of interest or stupidity. The child's ability to look his thought, appropriate manners, demonstrative gestures, will help him on his way through a world of seeing men. There are many sightless men who try hard and work faithfully, but who lack the accomplishments and amenities of social intercourse. They do not make friends readily and are much alone. Because they seem spiritless they are not invited out, and thus they do become that which they seem; uninteresting, dispirited, uncompanionable. The blind man's opportunities to mingle with his kind depend largely on whether as a child he has learned attractive ways and manners, on whether his mother has laughed with him and sung to him and let him feel with his hands her smile, her frown, her look of surprised delight. The seeing child observes these things unconsciously. To reveal them to the blind child a little conscious effort is necessary.

For, after all, the whole difference between training a blind child and one who sees lies in a little extra effort. The blind child cannot be deliberately stuffed with information and good morals. Directions must be taught him by indirections. He is a growing human thing, like all the other child-plants in the garden. Only he needs more care. He requires the gardener's best skill. He is to be encouraged, not forced. He can be coaxed, not compelled, to commit poems to memory, to reproduce stories and tell them to his playmates. This should be a pastime and a pleasure, and it will help his progress in composition and reading when he enters school. Throughout life he will find story-telling a welcome diversion for idle hours. Did you ever notice how few seeing people can tell a story? And yet they read so many! Would not a blind man who could tell a story be delightful company by the fireside? The world has not forgotten a blind man who told stories in Greece, centuries ago, or another who sat with closed eyes and read as upon a scroll within his brain the story of creation written anew. The princes and nobles of Japan have heard the wisdom of their ancestors and the history of their country from the eloquent lips of blind men.

There are so many fine and useful things that a blind man can do if he is well brought up, so many disagreeable and debilitating things that he will do if he is left untrained. Like other human beings, he must go forward or he will sink and fall. If his energies are not directed in childhood they will run wild into contortions and perversions. The child not drilled in deportment, not taught to use his hands, will fall into ungainly nervous habits called "blindisms." Left to himself he rocks his body, puts his fingers in his eyes, shakes his hands before his face, sways from one foot to the other, bends forward and back, and develops other uncouth mannerisms. These are frequent among blind children who enter the schools, and the fight to overcome them is much harder than would have been timely discipline at home. In a blind child it is important, first, to beware of bad habits, then to cultivate good ones.

The cultivation of good habits, of right moral and religious ideas, is a delicate and yet natural process. One method that is likely to succeed is to speak the pleasant word of praise at the right moment. Seeing people are subjected to unconscious criticism in the inevitable comparison they make between what they do and what others do. The blind person needs to be told more often and more definitely when he has done well and when he has done ill. Here the parent (and other seeing persons) should guard against the temptation to praise a blind child because he is afflicted. It is harmful, not helpful, to the sightless to be commended for work that is worthless. In this country good people have for years bought cheap beadwork and fancywork from the blind, not because they admired the articles, but because they pitied the makers. This has tended to keep the standard of work low. At present, however, efforts are being made in several States to raise the standard of work and give the blind opportunity to make useful and beautiful things.

It is wonderful what a wise mother can accomplish for her blind child, and the story I shall relate cannot fail to hearten those who have a disaster to right in the lives of their little ones. Dr. F. J. Campbell, who is himself blind, has done more than any other man living for the sightless. He is an American, born in Tennessee, and he founded and has managed for thirty years the Royal Normal College and Academy of Music for the Blind at Norwood, near London. He is a teacher and an exemplar of independence, self-reliance, and dignified industry for the blind. In vacation time, just to show what the blind can do he has climbed Mont Blanc, and in worktime he has educated and placed in positions of competence some of the best musicians of England. He lost his sight when he was between four and five years of age. At that time there were only two or three schools for the blind in America. His father said to the other members of the family: "Joseph will never see again. He is helpless. We must all work for him and take care of him. As long as he lives he must never want for anything that we can give him. We must wait on him and do everything for him."

The family agreed conscientiously — all but the mother. She took her blind son by the hand, led him into another room, and said: "Joseph, don't you pay any attention to what you have heard. You can learn to work, and I will teach you. In fact, you've got to work." She did teach him, and saw to it that he did what the other boys did. But what could a blind boy do? Once he suggested that he might chop kindling-wood for the fire. The father was unwilling to trust a blind boy with an axe. But soon he went away on business for a few days. Then the mother took the boy to the woodpile, gave him an axe and set him to work. When the father returned he found six cords of firewood cut and piled. "Well done, lads," he said to the other boys, and then they told him that Joseph had done it all. The father took the hint and bought the boy a new light axe, and from that time taught him all kinds of work about the farm.

Senator Gore, of Oklahoma, was stricken with blindness when he was eleven years old. His father told him that he must go to an institution for the blind. "No, Father," exclaimed the sturdy little lad, "I will go to school for the seeing, right here." They lived then in Mississippi. The boy was page in the State Senate, and boarded at the house of United States Senator George. So he was brought up in politics and early acquired the love for debating and oratory which led to his success in public life. Mr. Gore's State will not fail to build the fine institution for the blind which some of its citizens are planning, for the welfare of the sightless must be dear to the heart of young Oklahoma, the first American Commonwealth, I believe, to send a blind man to the national Senate.

Doctor Campbell and Senator Gore are men of unusual native power, but their success teaches us surely that ordinary blind children can by careful teaching be fitted for ordinary studies and pursuits. It is significant, I think, that Senator Gore did not go to an institution for the blind, and the question may be raised, though it cannot be easily settled, whether our blind children cannot be taken care of in the ordinary public schools. All the apparatus they need is raised books, raised maps, and a tablet to write on. These can be furnished as well at a regular school as at an institution. The teachers are overworked, it is true, and in the prevailing ignorance about the blind they would expect a blind child to be a difficult burden. But a special teacher could be engaged at less ultimate cost to the community than the cost of existing institutions. The advantage to the blind child would be great. He would be brought up in the midst of seeing children and become a familiar and accepted member of the community in which he must live and work. His presence in the school might have a good effect on popular education by proving that education is a process of mind, and not a matter of apparatus. Solving mathematical problems in his head, he would suggest perhaps to his teachers that arithmetic is an abstraction, and is independent of chalk and blackboard, even of the newest textbook recommended by the school committee.

The reason for the institutions lies in the history of education, not in the essential needs of the blind. Philanthropists saw years ago that blind children were neglected — left out of the race entirely. The first thought, naturally, was to bring them together, in a special institution. So one State after another built its school for the blind, and their education remained a mystery to the general public, surrounded, like most institutional education, by myth and superstition. Even now some parents shrink from sending their afflicted children to an "institution," for the very word suggests a prison or asylum. Under present conditions no parent should deprive a blind child of such opportunities as the schools for the blind afford. The children are well treated, they are not coddled, their blindness is not emphasized, and much is done to make them happy.

Whatever the formal schooling of a blind child is to be, his preliminary training and the use he makes of his education depend largely upon his mother. Before he is ready for school she can send to the nearest institution, get an alphabet sheet of embossed characters and teach him his letters. There is the same eagerness for knowledge among blind children as among seeing. Blind boys and girls long to read as their seeing brothers and sisters do. They finger the schoolbooks that the others are studying and feel the blank pages to find the stories that are being read aloud. The first signs of intellectual curiosity will be met by the watchful mother, and she will make her blind child ready for the school that must ere long educate him, ready for the long road of life on which he must set out through the darkness.

A Letter to Mark Twain

Read by Mark Twain at a meeting of the New York Association for the Blind; March 29, 1906.

My Dear Mr. Clemens:

It is a great disappointment to me not to be with you and the other friends who have joined their strength to uplift the blind. The meeting in New York will be the greatest occasion in the movement which has so long engaged my heart, and I regret keenly not to be present and feel the inspiration of living contact with such an assembly of wit, wisdom, and philanthropy.

I should be happy if I could have spelled into my hand the words as they fall from your lips, and receive, even as it is uttered, the eloquence of our newest ambassador to the blind. We have not had such advocates before.

My disappointment is softened by the thought that never at any meeting was the right word so sure to be spoken. But superfluous as all other appeal must seem after you and Mr. Choate have spoken, nevertheless, as I am a woman, I cannot be silent, and I ask you to read this letter, knowing that it will be lifted to eloquence by your kindly voice.

To know what the blind man needs, you who can see must imagine what it would be not to see, and you can imagine it more vividly if you remember that before your journey's end you may have to go the dark way yourself. Try to realize what blindness means to those whose joyous activity is stricken to inaction.

It is to live long, long days — and life is made up of days. It is to live immured, baffled, impotent, all God's world shut out. It is to sit helpless, defrauded, while your spirit strains and tugs at its fetters and your shoulders ache for the burden they are denied, the rightful burden of labour.

The seeing man goes about his business confident and self-dependent. He does his share of the work of the world in mine, in quarry, in factory, in counting-room, asking of others no boon save the opportunity to do a man's part and to receive the labourer's guerdon.

In an instant accident blinds him. The day is blotted out. Night envelops all the visible world. The feet which once bore him to his task with firm and confident stride stumble and halt and fear the forward step. He is forced to a new habit of idleness, which like a canker consumes the mind and destroys its beautiful faculties.

Memory confronts him with his lighted past. Amid the tangible ruins of his life as it promised to be he gropes his pitiful way. You have met him on your busy thoroughfares, with faltering feet and outstretched hands, patiently dredging the universal dark, holding out for sale his petty wares, or his cap for your pennies; and this was a man with ambitions and capabilities.

It is because we know that these ambitions and capabilities can be fulfilled that we are working to improve the condition of the adult blind. You cannot bring back sight to the vacant eyes; but you can give a helping hand to the sightless along their dark pilgrimage. You can teach them new skill. For work they once did with the aid of their eyes you can substitute work that they can do with their hands.

They ask only opportunity, and opportunity is the torch of darkness. They crave no charity, no pension, but the satisfaction that comes from lucrative toil, and this satisfaction is the right of every human being.

At your meeting New York will speak its word for the blind, and when New York speaks, the world listens. The true message of New York is not the commercial ticking of busy telegraphs, but the mightier utterances of such gatherings as yours.

Of late our periodicals have been filled with depressing revelations of great social evils. Querulous critics have pointed to every flaw in our civic structure. We have listened long enough to the pessimists.

You once told me you were a pessimist, Mr. Clemens; but great men are usually mistaken about themselves. You are an optimist. If you were not, you would not preside at the meeting. For it is an answer to pessimism. It proclaims that the heart and the wisdom of a great city are devoted to the good of mankind, that in this, the busiest city in the world, no cry of distress goes up but receives a compassionate and generous answer. Rejoice that the cause of the blind has been heard in New York, for the day after it shall be heard around the world.

The Heaviest Burden of the Blind

Address before the New York Association for the Blind, January 15, 1907.

It is a great pleasure to me to speak in New York about the blind. For New York is great because of the open hand with which it responds to the needs of the weak and the poor. The men and women for whom I speak are poor and weak in that they lack one of the chief weapons with which the human being fights his battle. But they must not on that account be sent to the rear. Much less must they be pensioned like disabled soldiers. They must be kept in the fight for their own sake, and for the sake of the strong. It is a blessing to the strong to give help to the weak. Otherwise there would be no excuse for having the poor always with us.

The help we give the unfortunate must be intelligent. Charity may flow freely and yet fail to touch the deserts of human life. Disorganized charity is creditable to the heart but not to the mind. Pity and tears make poetry; but they do not raise model tenement houses, or save the manhood of blind men. The heaviest burden on the blind is not blindness, but idleness, and they can be relieved of this greater burden.

Our work for the blind is practical. The Massachusetts commission, your association, and the New York commission are placing it on a sincere basis. The first task is to make a careful census of the blind, to find out how many there are, how old they are, what are their circumstances, when they lost their sight and from what cause. Without such a census there can be no order in our work. In Massachusetts this task is nearly completed.

The next step is to awaken each town and city to a sense of its duty to the blind. For it is the community where the blind man lives that ultimately de-termines his success or his failure. The State can teach him to work, supply him with raw materials and capital to start his business; but his fellow-citizens must furnish the market for his products, and give him the encour-agement without which no blind man can make headway. They must do more than this: they must meet him with a sympathy that conforms to the dignity of his manhood and his capacity for service. Indeed, the community should regard it as a disgrace for the blind to beg on the street corner, or re-ceive unearned pensions.

It is not helpful — in the long run it is harmful — to buy worthless articles of the blind. For many years kind-hearted people have brought futile and childish things because the blind made them. Quantities of bead work, that can appeal to no eye save the eye of pity, have passed as specimens of the work of the blind. If bead work had been studied in the schools for the blind and supervised by competent seeing persons, it could have been made a profitable industry for the sightless. I have examined beautiful beadwork in the shops — purses, bags, belts, lamp-shades, and dress-trimmings — some of it very expensive — imported from France and Germany. Under proper supervision this beadwork could be made by the blind. This is only one example of the sort of manufacture that the blind may profitably engage in.

One of the principal objects of the movement which we ask you to help is to promote good workmanship among the sightless. In Boston, in a fashionable shopping district, the Massachusetts commission has opened a salesroom where the best handicraft of all the sightless in the State may be exhibited and sold. There are hand-woven curtains, table-covers, bed-spreads, sofa-pillows, linen suits, rugs; and the articles are of good design and workmanship. People buy them not out of pity for the maker, but out of admiration for the thing. Orders have already come from Minnesota, from England, from Egypt. So the blind of the New World have sent light into Egyptian darkness!

This shop is under the same roof with the salesroom of the Perkins Institution for the Blind. The old school and the new commission are working side by side. I desire to see similar cooperation between the New York Institution for the Blind and the New York Association. The true value of a school for the sightless is not merely to enlighten intellectual darkness, but to lend a hand to every movement in the interests of the blind. It is not enough that our blind children receive a common-school education. They should do something well' enough to become wage-earners. When they are properly educated, they desire to work more than they desire ease or entertainment. If some of the blind are ambitionless and lazy, the fault lies partly with those who have directed their education, partly with our indolent progenitors in the Garden of Eden. All over the land the blind are stretching forth eager hands to the new tasks which shall soon be within their reach. They embrace labour gladly because they know it is strength.

One of our critics has suggested that we who call the blind forth to toil are as one who should overload a disabled horse and compel him to earn his oats. In the little village where I live, there was a lady so mistakenly kind to a pet horse that she never broke him to harness, and fed him twelve quarts of oats a day. The horse had to be shot. I am not afraid that we shall kill our blind with kindness. I am still less afraid that we shall break their backs.

Nay, I can tell you of blind men who of their own accord enter the sharp competition of business and put their hands zealously to the tools of trade. It is our part to train them in business, to teach them to use their tools skilfully. Before this association was thought of, blind men had given examples of energy and industry, and with such examples shining in the dark other blind men will not be content to be numbered among those who will not, or cannot, carry burden on shoulder or tool in hand — those who know not the honour of hard-won independence.

The new movement for the blind rests on a foundation of common sense. It is not the baseless fabric of a sentimentalist's dream. We do not believe that the blind should be segregated from the seeing, gathered together in a sort of Zion City, as has been done in Roumania and attempted in Iowa. We have no queen to preside over such a city. America is a democracy, a multimonarchy, and the city of the blind is everywhere. Each community should take care of its own blind, provide employment for them, and enable them to work side by side with the seeing. We do not expect to find among the blind a disproportionate number of geniuses. Education does not develop in them remarkable talent. Like the seeing man, the blind man may be a philosopher, a mathematician, a linguist, a seer, a poet, a prophet. But believe me, if the light of genius burns within him, it will burn despite his infirmity, and not because of it. The lack of one sense — or two — never helped a human being. We should be glad of the sixth or the sixteenth sense with which our friends and the newspaper reporters, more generous than nature, are wont to endow us. To paraphrase Mr. Kipling, we are not heroes and we are not cowards too. We are ordinary folk limited by an extraordinary incapacity. If we do not always succeed in our undertakings, even with assistance from friends, we console ourselves with the thought that in the vast company of the world's failures is many a sound pair of eyes!

I appeal to you, give the blind man the assistance that shall secure for him complete or partial independence. He is blind and falters. Therefore go a little more than halfway to meet him. Remember, however brave and self-reliant he is, he will always need a guiding hand in his.

What to Do For the Blind

The *World's Work,* August, 1907.

The American people have been liberal in their gifts to the blind. Their attitude has been one of sincere interest and kindly expectation of success. There has been generous provision to educate the children and to surround the aged with comfort. Yet the truth forces itself upon those who study the problem that much remains to be done, that there is some important work which has not been even started in many of our States.

To begin at the beginning, we have found that much blindness is unnecessary, that perhaps a third of it is the result of disease which can be averted by timely treatment. Then the instruction of parents and friends in the care of blind children needs to be carried to every corner of the country. We have before us a long campaign of education to teach parents that they must encourage sightless children to romp and play and grow strong as their seeing brothers and sisters do. Failure to understand this, and the natural inclination to shield and pamper defective children impose upon the schools the unnecessary burden of straightening crooked backs and deformed limbs and correcting nervous habits, engendered by lack of intelligent discipline at home. The backward condition of the pupils when they enter the schools for the blind accounts in part for the failure of some of our institutions in the work they are intended to do. The failure is due partly to the inadequacy of the schools themselves. Thus we find need of improvement in training from babyhood to adult life; and finally we discover a large class of adult blind persons for whom, as yet, no provision has been made in most American communities.

The records recently gathered by investigators show that even the educated, industrious blind cannot earn their living without more special assistance than they now receive. They are so severely handicapped throughout life that they cannot shift for themselves. Even after careful training and apprenticeship, they still need help to find their place in the world of workers, a world which often does not believe that they can work. Step by step they must prove their ability. At the present time, thousands of such American men and women are living idle, dependent lives. The cause of their unproductive dependence is the error of not carrying their education far enough, and of not providing them with suitable employment. I can explain the situation by outlining what seems to be the main tendency of the education of the blind in Europe.

The effort there is to give them trades and handicrafts by means of which they can earn their bread, or part of it. The aim of the best European education is to make each individual self-supporting. The blind require special teaching to enable them to use the senses of hearing and touch in the place of sight, to live and toil in the dark.

When philanthropists first approach the problem, they expect that education will develop in the blind extraordinary mental capacities. They reason that blind persons, shut out from everyday distractions, will enjoy great concentration of mind, and as a result will be poets, musicians, and thinkers. Such was the dream of Valentin Haüy in France and Dr. S. G. Howe in Boston, and such to-day is the dream of the good Queen of Roumania. But experience taught Haüy and Howe that the poets, the musicians, and the philosophers were not forthcoming. We have to deal with a miscellaneous class of defective persons who are often not only blind, but weak from the very cause that destroyed their sight. From confinement and want of exercise they are often deficient in vitality and dulled in mind. In such conditions of body and mind genius can hardly flourish. It is true that blind men sometimes have the divine spark in them. They have become distinguished in art, in science, in literature. But whatever eminence they have attained has been in spite of their misfortune, and not because of it. The great exceptions cheer and encourage us; but they remain exceptions. The question is, what shall be done with the uninspired majority?

In Europe it was soon found that the wisest course is not to direct their instruction wholly toward things of the intellect, but provide trades and industries by means of which they can earn a livelihood. The more advanced schools of Europe try to give them an education suited to their common intelligence and their uncommon infirmity, and the work of the schools is supplemented and made practical by societies which help them to put their education to the best use as ordinary, industrious, self-respecting citizens. The vicissitudes of business are so complicated that they easily miss their few chances of self-support, unless they have special organizations to find positions for them, to advertise their abilities and persuade the community to give the blind musician, or teacher, or broom-maker, or masseur, or whatever he may be, profitable employment. There are such organizations in Europe that use every effort to bring industrial training within the reach of all the blind, and are the channels through which the true end of education and charity for the sightless is achieved.

In America, where the struggle for existence is less severe, and where money is more plentiful, we have been long coming to realize the necessity of fitting each individual for a self-supporting life. Our education has been administered to all children alike, without regard for their capacities or circumstances. Consequently most children leave school unprepared for a trade or industry or profession. This general state of American education has complicated the difficulties of the sightless. Excellent schools for their instruction, established on sound principles, have existed since 1832 when the first institutions for the blind were opened in Boston and New York. But they have laid little or no stress upon industrial training. Their system of education has the same faults as that in the ordinary American schools for the seeing. Besides, our institutions for the blind are intended for children and youths, and have not taken very much interest in the adults. Until recently we have had nothing which corresponds to the societies for the blind in Europe, and the associations which have lately been formed in two or three American states are scarcely beyond the stage of tentative effort.

One great difficulty of the adult blind is, that of the thousands of occupations in which men engage, only a very few will ever be possible for the sightless. The occupations in which they have already succeeded are the manufacture of mattresses, brooms, brushes, mats, baskets, some simple kinds of carpentry and weaving, cobbling, typewriting, piano-tuning, massage, knitting, crocheting, and plain sewing. They have also succeeded to some extent as travelling salesmen and agents. There is opportunity for them in newsstands, tobacco and candy shops and other small businesses. No doubt other occupations and industries will be found for them.

But even a few occupations are sufficient for them all, if the trade and the man are fitted one to the other, and both are properly advanced in the hurrying market-place of life. The practical failure of many graduates of our schools for the blind is rooted in the entire problem of education. But in addition to these there is a class whose problem is not strictly educational — those who have lost their sight in mature years.

The lot of an idle graduate of a school who has learned how to be blind is hard enough. He leaves school flushed with hope and courage. He thinks he can brave the world and conquer it. Perhaps he hears of a position as teacher and makes the necessary application. His application is refused because he cannot see. He learns of another position and applies for it in person, passes all the tests and examinations successfully, and is praised for his ability. Still his services are not accepted because it is not thought possible for him to teach even music as well as a seeing man. Yet he has been fitted to teach music. He has even studied under masters.

If a young blind man, educated and trained in the dark, loses courage after repeated failure, what must be the feelings of one who is suddenly stricken blind in mine or factory? Blighted ambitions, sorrow, bitterness, and despair. "What will become of me? Who will feed and clothe my little ones? Must I live useless always, an object of charity?" These are the questions that rack him. He may try to be cheerful; but happy he cannot be, unless he finds occupation. His unused faculties will rust. The light of intelligence fades from his countenance. His hands grope for the tool that accident has snatched away.

What shall we do to alter this condition of the blind in America? First of all, it is necessary to awaken public interest in matters concerning the sightless. An enlightened public sentiment is the only power in a democracy that can bring about and maintain the betterment of my class. When the public understands the blind man, his needs and capacities, there will be an end to the more special causes which we find partly responsible for present conditions in this country — lack of enthusiasm, intelligence, and cooperation on the part of those who have charge of the institutions for the blind.

The superintendents of these institutions, dependent on boards of trustees who know almost nothing about the needs of these institutions and the difficulties of the blind, trusted by a public which is not informed, are often men of indifferent attainment, wedded to petty theories, and unprogressive. They are generally kind, and believe that they have the best interests of their charges at heart. But the existing condition of the sightless throughout the country affords sufficient evidence of their incompetence.

An obvious illustration of their incompetency and the absence of cooperation between the schools is the confusion in the prints for the blind. One would think that the advantages of having a common print would not require argument. Yet every effort to decide which print is best has failed. The Perkins Institution for the Blind, with a large printing fund, clings to Line Letter — embossed characters, shaped like Roman letters, [1] in spite of the fact that most of the blind prefer a point system. The Pennsylvania Institution for the Blind offers its readers American Braille, a print in which the letters are composed of raised dots. This is a modification of the system which was perfected by Louis Braille three quarters of a century ago and is still the system used throughout Europe. The New York Institution invented, controls, and advocates New York Point, another species of Braille. The money appropriated by the national government to emboss books for the blind is used for all the types. The new periodical, the *Matilda Ziegler Magazine for the Blind,* the boon for which we have waited many years, is printed in American Braille and New York Point. The same book, expensive to print once, has to be duplicated in the various systems for the different institutions. Other prints are yet to come. They are still in the crucible of meditation. A plague upon all these prints! Let us have one system, whether it is an ideal one, or not. For my part, I wish nothing had been invented except European Braille. There was already a considerable library in this system when the American fever for invention plunged us into this Babel of prints which is typical of the many confusions from which the blind suffer throughout the United States.

We Americans spend more money on the education of defectives than any other country. But we do not always find the shortest, easiest, and most economical way of accomplishing the end we have in view. We desire to bring the greatest happiness to the largest number. We give generously as earnest of our desire, and then we do not see that our bounty is wisely spent.

Three or four years ago, in New York, two cultivated women became interested in the blind. They observed how much pleasure some blind persons derived from a musical entertainment, and they thought how many hours the sightless must spend without diversion. They set to work to establish a bureau for the distribution to the blind of tickets for the theatre, the opera, and other entertainments. This brought them into contact with the blind, and they soon perceived that their efforts to entertain them were but to gild a sepulchre. The blind said to them: "You are very kind to give us pleasure. But it is work we need, something to do with our hands. It is terrible to sit idle all day long. Give us that wondrous thing, interest in life. Work wedded to interest gives dignity, sweetness, and strength even to our kind of life."

The two noble women determined to see what could be done. They went for information to the New York Institution for the Blind. They asked why the blind were unemployed. They received courteous assurances that everything possible was being done for the blind, that their hard lot was the inevitable result of circumstances. The fact that they were idle was deplored, but there was no help for it. In a world of machinery, specialized industry, and keen competition the blind man could not expect to find profitable occupation. He must, it was urged, ever remain a public charge to be treated kindly, and the young women were heartily commended for their efforts to supply them with entertainment. Indeed, it was argued, it would be cruel to add to the burden of infirmity the burden of labour. It would be quite as cruel to expect them to earn their living as to compel a disabled horse to earn his oats. (The same kind of specious argument was being disseminated in Massachusetts and other States.) But the ladies were too intelligent and too earnest to be convinced. Their visit was the beginning of a new movement in New York toward the betterment of the sightless.

Soon afterward an association was formed. Meetings were held. Men of ability and eloquence spoke in behalf of the work and drove the truth home to the people that the heaviest burden upon the blind is not blindness, but idleness. The Institution raised its head in protest and self-justification, and tried to prejudice the blind against the association. It opposed an adequate census of the sightless. The association appealed to the Legislature for an appropriation to carry on the census. The Legislature made the appropriation and established a commission. The commission appointed one of the two ladies Director of the Census, with the result that a complete registry of the blind of New York State will soon be available. This census will not be like the United States census figures, which are vague and incomplete, but will tell how many blind there are, where each live, and in what circumstances, what occupation he has, what trade he has learned in school, how old he is, how long he has been blind, and from what cause he lost his sight. The New York census and the Massachusetts census will tell with scientific definiteness what has been left undone, and will enable us to deal more intelligently with the problems of the sightless.

The Massachusetts Commission for the Blind grew out of a volunteer organization which carried on investigations and experiments. At the experiment station a few blind persons learned to weave rugs, fabrics suitable for curtains, table covers, and sofa pillows, and other things useful and beautiful. At this station industries and processes were tested with a view to increase the number of lucrative occupations in which the blind, especially women, might engage. After it had demonstrated to the State that they are capable of higher efficiency than they have generally reached, the association asked the Legislature for an appropriation to extend the work. The appropriation was granted, and a commission was appointed by the Governor to be responsible for the welfare of all the blind in Massachusetts.

The commission took over all the work of the association, proceeded with the census, enlarged the experiment plant, opened an attractive shop in a fashionable shopping district of Boston, and will open industrial shops in other parts of the State as seems advisable. The commission furnishes blind home-workers with raw materials. It starts trustworthy blind men and women in business, with the understanding that if they succeed, they will pay back the amount the State has lent them. The commission gives information to sightless persons who seek positions. Above all things, it urges upon each community its responsibility for the care and employment of the blind within its precincts. State institutions can train the blind man: but his fellow-citizens must furnish the market for his products, and see to it that he gets his fair share of patronage.

In Massachusetts, happily, opposition between the old order and the new has ceased. The Perkins Institution for the Blind and the commission are working together. The shop where the commission puts on sale the work of the sightless is under the same roof with the salesroom of the Perkins Institution. The school in changing its attitude has set an example which other institutions cannot afford to disregard. For the new movement in behalf of the blind will not cease until every sightless person in our land has the chance to earn at least part of his support.

Philanthropists and public-spirited people all over the country have taken up the work. Business men are advocating it. Great men like Mark Twain and Mr. Choate have approved it. Governors and legislatures have given it public sanction. Its complete success now depends on three classes of responsible persons: First, the directors of the institutions and other educators; second, the trustees of the institutions and the State Boards; third, and ultimately, the public, of which the blind man is one.

We ask that the directors be cultivated men, sincerely interested in the whole problem; that if they have not the initiative to lead the way to progress, they will accept and carry out intelligent suggestions. We ask that the trustees of our institutions for the blind be chosen for the highest interest of the sightless, for their competency, and not merely for name, family or social eminence. We ask that they be men who can afford a little time to study the problems of the blind. We ask that the trustees be so qualified that no director or teacher or any other person can impose upon them as to the condition, work or efficiency of the school, or the accomplishments of its graduates. We ask that the trustees build schools for the blind on land suited to the peculiar needs of the sightless.

The blind need to be placed where they can have plenty of room for playgrounds and learn a little of farming and gardening. Willow-work is one of the well-known industries for the blind in Europe; but it has not been introduced here, except in Wisconsin, because of the lack of willow. Why not plant willow on land near the institutions, and employ blind people to trim and care for the willow groves? Why not let the blind raise poultry? It has proved a profitable industry for them in England. If these suggestions do not prove practical, the fact remains that the sightless need large playgrounds — out-of-door life. Their inactivity and often the disease which caused their blindness keep them undeveloped and anemic. If they are to become strong, healthy men and women, they must have a great deal of unrestrained exercise in the open air. In the old days there was at least an excuse for putting the institution in the cities; but now, when the trolley makes the country accessible, every consideration of economy and well-being for the sightless cries out against a school for the blind in a crowded city.

We ask the public to take all these matters to heart and understand the needs of the sightless. The strangest ignorance exists in the minds of people as to what the blind can do. They are amazed when they hear that a blind person can write on the typewriter, dress himself without assistance, go up and down stairs alone, eat with a fork, and know when the sun is shining. But they are ready to believe that we have a special stock of senses to replace those which we have lost! They believe unquestioningly, for instance, that I can play the piano, distinguish colours and write sonnets in two or three languages. Yet they doubt that I can write this article, or arrive at the simple facts and deductions it contains.

The public must learn that the blind man is neither a genius nor a freak nor an idiot. He has a mind which can be educated, a hand which can be trained, ambitions which it is right for him to strive to realize, and it is the duty of the public to help him to make the best of himself, so that he can win light through work.

[1] Line letter is no longer printed at the Perkins Institution. The present superintendent, Mr. Allen, is a progressive man and an advocate of American Braille.

The Unemployed Blind
(a later view)

Editorial from the *Ziegler Magazine for the Blind,* April, 1911.

Some time ago I received a pathetic letter from a workman in a woollen mill. I quote a part of it:

"I was employed in the worsted trade in England before coming to this country. I had worked for ten years and had learnt a good deal about wool, tops, and noils. I came to this country in the hope of climbing the industrial ladder. I could hear pretty well, or I should not have passed the immigration officers. I got work quickly at the very bottom of the ladder. I kept my eyes open and learnt everything that came my way, and in time I was transferred to the combing room to learn to be section hand. By this time my hearing had become slightly worse. All the help in this department were either Italians or Poles, so that between their broken English and my defective hearing I was much handicapped. I have been on short time for over a year, and since the New Year I have earned $6.71 per week. There are six of us to feed, clothe, shelter, and coal to buy. How to find a bare existence is the problem that confronts me to-day. I would take anything where I could earn steady pay. I have the idea that I shall yet rise out of the mire. But in the meantime I must live and support my family, and this I cannot do under present circumstances."

This workman is deaf, but his position is similar to that of many of the sightless. We have been accustomed to regard the unemployed deaf and blind as victims of their infirmities. That is to say, we have supposed that if their sight and hearing were miraculously restored, they would find work. The problem of the underpaid and underemployed workman is too large to discuss here. But I wish to suggest to the readers of this article that the unemployment of the blind is only part of a greater problem.

There are, it is estimated, a million labourers out of work in the United States. Their inaction is not due to physical defects or lack of ability or of intelligence, or to ill health or vice. It is due to the fact that our present system of production necessitates a large margin of idle men. The business world in which we live cannot give every man opportunity to fulfil his capabilities or even assure him continuous occupation as an unskilled labourer. The means of employment — the land and the factories, that is, the tools of labour — are in the hands of a minority of the people, and are used rather with a view to increasing the owner's profits than with a view to keeping all men busy and productive. Hence there are more men than "jobs." This is the first and the chief evil of the so-called capitalistic system of production. The workman has nothing to sell but his labour. He is in strife, in rivalry with his fellows for a chance to sell his power. Naturally the weaker workman is thrust aside. That does not mean that he is utterly incapacitated for industrial activity, but only that he is less capable than his successful competitor.

In the majority of cases there is no relation between unemployment and ability. A factory shuts down, and all the operatives, the more competent as well as the less competent, are thrown out of work. In February the cotton mill owners of Massachusetts agreed to run the mills on a schedule of four days a week. The employees were not to blame for the reduction of work, nor were the employers to blame. The conditions of the market compelled it.

Thus, it has come to pass that in this land of plenty there is an increasing number of "superfluous men." The doors of industry are closed to them the whole year or part of the year. No less than six million American men, women, and children are in a permanent state of want because of total or partial idleness. In a small corner of this vast social distress we find our unemployed blind. Their lack of sight is not the primary cause of their idleness; it is a contributing cause; it relegates them to the enormous army of the unwillingly idle.

We can subsidize the work of the sightless; we can build special institutions and factories for them, and solicit the help of wealthy patrons. But the blind man cannot become an independent, self-supporting member of society, he can never do all that he is capable of, until all his seeing brothers have opportunity to work to the full extent of their ability. We know now that the welfare of the whole people is essential to the welfare of each. We know that the blind are not debarred from usefulness solely by their infirmity. Their idleness is fundamentally caused by conditions which press heavily upon all working people, and deprive hundreds of thousands of good men of a livelihood.

I recommend that all who are interested in the economic problem of the sightless study the economic problem of the seeing. Let us begin with such books as Mr. Robert Hunter's "Poverty," and Edmond Kelly's "Twentieth Century Socialism." Let us read these books, not for "theory," as it is sometimes scornfully called, but for facts about the labour conditions of America. Mr. Kelly was a teacher of political economy, a lecturer on municipal government at Columbia University. Mr. Hunter has spent many years studying the American workman in his home and in the shop. The facts which they spread before us show that it is not physical blindness, but social blindness which cheats our hands of their right to toil.

The Education of the Deaf

Address before the International Otological Congress, at the Harvard Medical School, August 16, 1912.

I am glad that this congress of doctors is going to give some time to the problem of the deaf, to the problem that must be solved, not by surgery, but by education. You have devoted yourselves nobly to the study of the organ of hearing and to the treatment of its diseases. But those whom you could not help, and who therefore ceased to be your patients — you have left them to the school-teacher. You have done splendid work in the laboratory and the consulting room; but you have not usually followed your patient into the schoolroom and into the paths of life where he is part of the human throng. You have not shown much interest in his efforts to understand the speech of men and to make his own speech intelligible.

This gathering is an indication that your interest will henceforth embrace the deaf pupil and the deaf citizen as well as the diseased ear, that you will cooperate with the teacher, that, in words of Dr. James Kerr Love, you will "raise the deaf child to the rank of a patient," I am very grateful, to you, gentlemen. This is a new day in the education of the deaf — the day when the physician is no longer content to fight the hostile silences with medicine and surgical instruments alone, but helps the teacher to pour the blessed waters of speech into the desert of dumbness.

The physician of olden times had no duty but to heal wounds and give medicine. It was his function to make sick people well. The modern physician is labouring to keep mankind well. He is a sanitary engineer, a sociologist, a constructive philanthropist. I am but urging you in the direction which your profession has already taken, when I ask you to look beyond the deaf ear to the deaf child, to the human being whose problem it is to recover, despite deafness, his golden birthright of spoken words. You will look behind the closed doors of sense and see the impatient spirit waiting to be set free. It will become your painful duty to tell the parents that their child will never hear. Resist the tendency — some physicians call it humane, I call it barbarous — of leaving the patient in hope of ultimate recovery when you know that it is impossible. I have heard of doctors who continued to prescribe useless remedies, such as electricity and osteopathy and even Christian Science, when they knew that there was no hope, simply because they had not the courage to tell the truth. Such kindness is expensive consolation. It would be much more to the point to prepare the unfortunate one for his fate, to help him arrange his life in anticipation of the changed conditions under which he must henceforth live.

I was about six years old before any of the specialists whom my parents consulted was brave enough to tell them that I should never see or hear. It was Doctor Chisholm of Baltimore who told them my true condition. "But," said he, "she can be educated," and he advised my father to take me to Washington and consult Doctor Alexander Graham Bell as to the best method of having me taught. Doctor Chisholm did exactly the right thing. My father followed his advice at once, and within a month I had a teacher, and my education was begun. From that intelligent doctor's office I passed from darkness to light, from isolation to friendship, companionship, knowledge. The parent who brings his child to your office, to your hospitals, should find in you, not a teacher, perhaps, but one who understands how far it is possible to right the disaster of deafness.

You should know about such work as that of my friend Mr. John D. Wright. When you know about the work that he and his teachers are doing, you will not be satisfied until every deaf child within your knowledge receives oral instruction.

How splendid it will be, what new courage we shall feel, if all aural surgeons henceforth use their influence to secure for every deaf child the opportunity to speak! The deaf and the teachers of the deaf need your help, and I am sure that you will help them in all the countries of the world from this day forth. Gentlemen, I thank you.

The Gift of Speech

Address before the German Scientific Society of New York, April 8, 1913.

I am glad that so many intelligent people are interested in helping the deaf to speak. You have asked me to come here and tell you how you can help in a work that is near to my heart. I am happy to stand before you, myself an example of what may be done to open dumb lips and liberate mute voices. I was dumb, now I speak. Intelligent instruction and the devotion of others wrought this miracle in me. What has been done for me can be done for others. You can all help the deaf child. You can help him by being interested in his struggle. You know now, if you have not known before, that he can learn to speak, and you can spread the knowledge that shall save him.

What the world needs is enlightened understanding on many subjects. There are plenty of brains and plenty of goodwill in the world. All that we need is to put them together. We must put thought and understanding into our efforts to help people. So much time and money are wasted every day because we do not get to the root of our difficulties!

In the case of the deaf, physicians and parents often retard the development of deaf children because they do not realize the necessity of an early start. When the physician knows that the organ of hearing is permanently impaired, the child should be placed under the guidance of a skilful teacher, even while there may still be hope of improvement. Nothing can be lost by beginning his education at once. Should he be fortunate enough to recover his hearing later, in the meantime the years will have been well spent educationally. If lifelong deafness is his lot, he will have had the advantages of a prompt beginning. The psychological period for the acquisition of speech and language will not have been lost, and the difficulty of teaching him will be lessened, and the result will be far more satisfactory.

Speech is the birthright of every child. It is the deaf child's one fair chance to keep in touch with his fellows. In many ways deafness is a greater disaster than blindness. Blindness robs the day of its light and makes us dependent and physically helpless. Deafness stops up the fountain-head of knowledge and turns life into a desert. For without language intellectual life is impossible. Try to imagine what it means to be deaf and dumb. Perpetual silence, silence full of longing to be understood, to speak, to hear the voices of our loved ones; silence that starves the mind, fetters the spirit and adds still another burden to labour.

Deafness, like poverty, stunts and deadens its victims, until they do not realize the wretchedness of their condition. They are incapable of desiring improvement. God help them! They grope, they stumble with their eyes wide open, they are indifferent. They miss everything in the world that makes life worth living, and yet they do not realize their own bondage. We must not wait for the deaf to ask for speech, or for the submerged of humanity to rise up and demand their liberties. We who see, we who hear, we who understand must help them, must give them the bread of knowledge, must teach them what their human inheritance is. Let every science do its part — medicine, surgery, otology, psychology, education, invention, economics, mechanics. And while you are working for the deaf child, do not forget that his problem is only part of a greater problem, the problem of bettering the condition of all mankind. Let us here and now resolve that every deaf child shall have a chance to speak, and that every man shall have a fair opportunity to make the best of himself. Then shall we mend the broken lyre of human speech and lessen the deafness and blindness of the world.

The Work of De L'Épée

Letter to the *Revue Générale de V Enseignement des Sourds-Muets,* Oct. 1912.

With my whole heart I join my deaf fellows in celebrating the two-hundredth anniversary of the birth of the Abbé de l'Épée. We celebrate not only his birthday, but also the soul-birthday of the deaf of France and of the entire world. As long as the memory of noble men remains upon earth, there shall be gladness because one was born who, with discerning love saw the bitter need of the deaf, dropped words of peace into the silence of their empty lives, and was a light to their stumbling feet.

I, too, was born again. I, too, have escaped the dread silence into which no message of love, no song of bird, no happy laugh may enter. I, too, have found my way back to the world of men and women, and the gates of knowledge have been flung wide for me. I rejoice in my restoration to the goodness of life.

How much more does it mean to me that thousands upon thousands of my deaf fellows have been taught, have been elevated to the lot of useful human beings! I am filled with tender gratitude to him who with his whole strength laboured that every deaf child might be educated and, despite his infirmity, become a happy worker in the world, adding his share to the common good.

How many devoted men and women have strengthened their hands unto this beautiful work where but one struggling thinker once stood before the world, and preached to the incredulous the gospel of education for the deaf.

1712-1912! What a change, what a transformation in the lot of the deaf, and in the methods of their instruction! Two hundred years ago they had no friend, no helper, no teacher, no school. Now, behold, they are being taught the wide world over from China to America and from the shores of the Indian Ocean to the far north. Behold the thousands who teach and learn, who labour with new methods, new devices, that they may find new roads to a richer life for the deaf,

Before De l'Épée the cause of the deaf was no cause at all. To-day it is not only their cause, but a public cause to which many feel it a great honour to consecrate their lives. Truly this is a day of joy — the joy of the deaf who can speak, or who, if mute, yet weave sweet words of kinship between themselves and humanity, a joy in which the burden of silence and isolation is forgotten. This is a festival of glad memories, a celebration of all the years in which darkened minds have been filled with the light of knowledge. Only De l'Épée's own work can fittingly be offered as a token of remembrance, a song of praise to our noble benefactor.

Let us then lift up our once mute voices and our once useless hands in witness to the enduring might of his example and his achievement. To-day we stand triumphant at the harvest of patient work. But we cannot celebrate the Abbe's birthday fittingly in one day. The true celebration must be a work ever-increasing and more efficient, a work ever-progressive, not limited to ideas of the past.

May all the deaf and their friends realize this. May they unite, animated by one idea — the betterment of the condition of the deaf. This is more important than any one's theories or methods of instruction. May this work be carried forward with unrelaxing vigour, until a day comes when no deaf child shall be left untaught, no deaf man or woman left unhelped.

The Message of Swedenborg

Introduction to a volume of Selections from Swedenborg, published in Braille at the Perkins Institution.

Swedenborg's works are full of stimulating faith, of confidence in what the author declares he has seen, heard, and touched. We who are blind are often glad that another's eye finds a road for us in a wide, perplexing darkness. How much more should we rejoice when a man of vision discovers a way to the radiant outer lands of the spirit! To our conception of God, the Word, and the Hereafter which we have received on trust from ages of unproved faith, Swedenborg gives a new actuality which is as startling, as thrilling as the angel-sung tidings of the Lord's birth. He brings fresh testimony to support our hope that the veil shall be drawn from unseeing eyes, that the dull ear shall be quickened, and dumb lips gladdened with speech.

Here, and now, our misfortune is irreparable. Our service to others is limited. Our thirst for larger activity is unsatisfied. The greatest workers for the race — poets, artists, men of science — men with all their faculties, are at times shaken with a mighty cry of the soul, a longing more fully to body forth the energy, the fire, the richness of fancy and of humane impulse which overburden them. What wonder, then, that we with our more limited senses and more humble powers should with a passionate desire crave wider range and scope of usefulness? Swedenborg says that "the perfection of man is the love of use," or service to others. Our groping acts are mere stammering suggestions of the greatness of service that we intend. We will to do more than we ever can do, and it is what we will that is in very truth ourselves. The dearest of all the consolations which Swedenborg's message brings to me is that in the next world our narrow field of work shall grow limitlessly broad and luminous. There the higher self that we long to be shall find realization.

Swedenborg, the man, was as lofty and noble as his work. He was one of those intellectual giants who astonish the world not oftener than once in a century with the vastness of their learning and their multitudinous activity. He was philosopher and theologian, and he was versed in the science of his time. He was a practical servant of the Swedish government, an inspector of mines, a metallurgist and engineer. The great mystic, then, was not a recluse, but an active man of the world. His life was serene, strong, gracious, moving with great ease under an incredible burden of work that would have broken the mental power of any ordinary man. Emerson says of him: "A colossal soul, he lies vast abroad on his times, uncomprehended by them, and requires a long focal distance to be seen."

His theological teachings are in many long volumes. Yet his central doctrine is simple. It consists of three main ideas: God as divine love, God as divine wisdom, and God as power for use. These ideas come as waves from an ocean which floods every bay and harbour of life with new potency of will, of faith, and of effort.

Love is the all-important doctrine. This love means not a vague, aimless emotion, but desire of good united with wisdom and fulfilled in right action. For a life in the dark this love is the surest guidance.

The difficulties which blindness throws across our path are grievous. We encounter a thousand restraints, and like all human beings we seem at times to be accidents and whims of fate. The thwarting of our deep-rooted instincts makes us feel with special poignancy the limitations that beset mankind. Swedenborg teaches us that love makes us free, and I can bear witness to its power of lifting us out of the isolation to which we seem to be condemned. When the idea of an active, all-controlling love lays hold of us, we become masters, creators of good, helpers of our kind. It is as if the dark had sent forth a star to draw us to Heaven. We discover in ourselves many undeveloped resources of will and thought. Checked, hampered, failing and failing again, we yet rise above the barriers that bound and confine us; our lives put on serenity and order. In love we find our release from the evils of physical and mental blindness. Our lack of sight forbids our hands to engage in many of the noblest human acts, but love is open to us, and as Swedenborg shows, love teaches us the highest of all arts — the art of living. From his writings we learn how to foster, direct, and practise this restoring love, this constructive, fertile faith, which is the yearning of man toward God.

Christmas in the Dark

The *Ladies' Home Journal,* December, 1906

When I was a little girl I spent the Christmas holidays one year at the Perkins Institution for the Blind. Some of the children, whose homes were far away, or who had no homes, had remained at the school. I have never known a merrier Christmas than that.

I hear some one ask: "What pleasure can Christmas hold for children who cannot see their gifts or the sparkling tree or the ruddy smile of Santa Claus?" The question would be answered if you had seen that Christmas of the blind children. The only real blind person at Christmas-time is he who has not Christmas in his heart. We sightless children had the best of eyes that day in our hearts and in our finger-tips. We were glad from the child's necessity of being happy. The blind who have outgrown the child's perpetual joy can be children again on Christmas Day and celebrate in the midst of them who pipe and dance and sing a new song!

For ten days before the holiday I was never still a single moment. I would be one of the party that went Christmasing. I laid my hands on everything that offered itself in the shops, and insisted on buying whatever I touched, until my teacher's eyes could not follow my fingers. How she ever kept me within the bounds of the fitness of things, maintained the scale of values, and overtook the caprices of my fancy, is matter of amazement. To the prettiest doll I would adhere a moment, then discover a still prettier one, and by decision the more perplex her and myself. At last the presents were selected and brought home.

Next, a great Christmas tree, a cedar which towered above my head, was brought to the house where the children lived and planted in the middle of the parlour. Preparation kept us busy for a week. I helped to hang wreaths of holly in the windows and over pictures, and had my share in trimming the tree. I ascended and descended continually on the ladder to tie on little balls, apples, oranges, cornucopias, strings of popcorn and festoons of tinsel. Then we attached the little tapers which should set the tree aglow. Last came the gifts. As we placed one and then another, it became more and more difficult for my fingers to thread their way in and out between the candles, the dangling balls, and the swinging loops of corn and tinsel, to find a secure position for the gifts. It seemed as if the green, sweet-scented branches must break with the burden of love-offerings heaped upon them, and soon the higher branches did begin to bend alarmingly with each heavier bundle, "like the cliff-swallow's nest, most like to fall when fullest."

One of the last gifts I hung in the midst of the thick branches was a most unseasonable and incongruous exotic — a toy cocoanut palm with a monkey, which had movable limbs, and which at the pressure of a spring would run up and slide down with a tiny cocoanut upon his head. Behold the miracle of toyland, a palm grafted upon a cedar! What matters botany? When a little girl wants anything to happen at Christmas, it happens and she is content.

Finally the tree was trimmed. Stars and crescents sparkled from branch to branch beneath my fingers, and farther up a large silver moon jostled the sun and stars. At the very top an angel with spread wings looked down on this wondrous, twinkling world — the child's Christmas world complete! But I think the stupendous view must have made him a little dizzy, for he kept turning slantwise and crosswise and anywise but the way a Christmas angel should float over a Christmas tree.

My teacher and the motherly lady who was matron in that house were children themselves; it really seemed as if there could not be a grave, experienced grown-up in the world. We admonished each other not to let fall a whisper of the mysteries that awaited the blind children, and for once I kept the whole matter at a higher value than a state secret.

On Christmas Eve I went to bed early, only to hop up many times to rearrange some package, to which I remembered I had not given the finishing touches, and to use all my powers of persuasion with the unruly angel, whom I invariably found in a reprehensible position.

Long before any one else was downstairs on Christmas morning, I took my last touch-look at the tree, and lo! the angel was correctly balanced, looking down in serene poise on the brilliant world below him. I suspected that Santa Claus had passed that way, and that under his discipline the angel, probably only a demi-angel, had been released from his sublunary infirmities. I turned to go, quite satisfied, when I discovered that Sadie's doll had shut her eyes on all the splendour that shone about her! "This will never do," I said — "sleeping at this time!" I poked her vigorously, until she winked, and finally, to show she was really awake, kicked Jupiter in the side, which disturbed the starry universe. But I had the planets in their orbits again before it was time for them to shine on the children.

After a hurried breakfast the blind children were permitted to enter the parlour and pass their hands over the tree. They knew instantly, without eyes, what a marvellous tree it was, filled with the good smells of June, filled with the songs of birds that had southward flown, filled with fruit that at the slightest touch tumbled into their laps. I felt them shout, I felt them dance up and down, and we all crowded about and hugged each other in rapture.

I distributed all the gifts myself and felt the gestures of delight as the children opened them. Very pretty gifts they were, well suited to sightless children. No disappointing picture-books, or paint-boxes, or kaleidoscopes, or games that require the use of sight. But there were many toys wonderful to handle, dolls, both boys and girls, including a real baby doll with a bottle in its mouth; chairs, tables, sideboards, and china sets, pincushions and workbaskets, little cases containing self -threading needles that the blind can use, sweet-scented handkerchiefs, pretty things to wear, and dainty ornaments that render children fair to look upon. Blind children, who cannot see, love to make themselves pretty for others to see.

There were animals, too, fierce lions and tigers, which proved that appearances are most deceptive, for when one took their heads off one found them full of sweet things. One girl had a bear that danced and growled whenever she wound a key somewhere in the region of its neck. Another had a cow that mooed when she turned its head.

The older children received books in raised print, not mournful, religious books, such as some good people see fit to choose for the sightless, but pleasant ones like "Undine," or Hawthorne's "Twice-Told Tales," or "The Story of Patsy," or "Alice in Wonderland." Fairy tales, novels, essays, books of travel and history, and magazines well filled with news of the world and gossipy articles are thumbed by the blind until the raised letters are worn down. Books of gloomy, depressing character, and many that are full of dry wisdom and no doubt very good for our morals, are likely to repose on the top shelf until the dust takes possession of them. The blind are rendered by their very affliction keenly alive to what is joyous and diverting. Their books are necessarily few, and most of them ought to be delightful and entertaining.

After we had touched our presents to our hearts' content we romped and frolicked as long as the little ones could go, and longer. If you had looked in on our unlagging merriment and had never seen blind children at play before, you might have been surprised that in our wildest gyrations we did not run into the tree, or knock over a chair, or fall into the fire that burned on the hearth. I think we must have looked like any other group of merry children.

You would have learned that the way to make the blind happy at Christmas, and all the time, is to treat them as far as possible like other persons. They do not like to be continually reminded of their blindness, set aside and neglected, or even waited on too much.

Had you been our guest you would have received a gift from the sightless, for they have one precious gift for the world. In their misfortune they are often happy, and in that they give an inspiring challenge to those who see. Shall any seeing man dare to be sad at Christmas or permit a little child to be other than merry and light-hearted? What can excuse the seeing from the duty and privilege of happiness while the blind child joins so merrily in the jubilee?

"Tiny Tim" was glad to be at church on Christmas because he thought the sight of him might remind folk who it was that gave the lame power to walk. Even so the blind may remind their seeing brethren who it was that opened the blinded eyes, unstopped the deaf ears, gave health to the sick, and knowledge to the ignorant, and declared that mightier things even than these shall be fulfilled. All the afflicted who keep the blessed day compel the affectionate thought that He abides with us yet.

The legend tells that when Jesus was born the sun danced in the sky, the aged trees straightened themselves and put on leaves and sent forth the fragrance of blossoms once more. These are the symbols of what takes place in our hearts when the Christ-Child is born anew each year. Blessed by the Christmas sunshine, our natures, perhaps long leafless, bring forth new love, new kindness, new mercy, new compassion. As the birth of Jesus was the beginning of the Christian life, so the unselfish joy at Christmas shall start the spirit that is to rule the new year.

A New Chime for the Christmas Bells

The *Metropolitan Magazine,* January, 1913.

Hear, oh, hear! The Christmas bells are ringing peal upon peal, chime upon chime! Full and clear they ring, and the air quivers with joy. What is the burden of their music as it floats far and wide? Awake! Awake! it says. A great Change is coming — peace upon earth, good-will to all men.

Together the bells and I call aloud, and we are not afraid! Peace upon earth, good-will to all men! Awake! Awake! We shall not rest again until good-will reigns, which is God's will done, nor shall we lie down until the voice of the angels is heard in all the circuits of the earth. We shall not slumber until light ariseth to all who sit in darkness, neither shall we sleep again until there is peace and gladness and content in the hearts of men. For a Great Change is coming, a wondrous Change, a World-change that shall fulfil all joy in a happy humanity.

Ring the Great Change, O Bells! Hear, oh, hear, all people! Long and confident the Christmas bells are ringing. Above our houses and through our open doors their voices fly. And they say: Awake! Awake! The night of man's captivity is at an end, the dawn of peace between man and man hasteneth to come and it shall not tarry!

The bells and I are strong with a new hope, vibrant with expectancy of this Great Change. Already men and women are working and thinking and living for this Great Change, and their efforts are mighty with the might of intelligence and good-will. For them the bells of a world-Christmas are ringing, and shall not cease with the brief hours of one glad day. Every day, every year, these men and women plan work, and dream, and their works are the heavenly message of the sweet-tongue bells!

Hear, oh, hear the bells! For ages the Christmas bells have rung their message of peace upon earth and good-will to all men. For ages they have summoned a sleeping world to a new life, a new ideal, a new joy. But too often they have sounded in ears sealed with ignorance. Too often has their glad news passed unheeded: "O children of men, your happiness lies but your will away from you. Unite, love, serve all, and ye shall grasp it."

Now, here and now, the bells and I will be heard! Not once a year, but from morning to morning we will be heard singing exultant, sure of our message. Let the sun pour its flood of light upon the land, or let the whole sky be dark, we will send our song up and down and all around, our song of the Great Change. Too long have men turned their faces from their tasks, from the needs of the common day, and fixed their eyes upon a better life sometime, somewhere. Too long have they dreamed of a distant life, instead of bringing that life into their earthly days. The Great Change ushers a true religion into the world, now and here — service for all men equally, devotion of each to the good of all alike.

Hear, oh, hear the Christmas bells as they greet the sun, the frost, the sailing cloud, the roving wind! Are they not the bells of your childhood's dearest joy, the bells of your brightest memories, the bells of your highest hope? Do they not voice your silent, baffled wish that all things shall be made new, that there shall be no more cramped, darkened lives, no more cruel customs, no more misery which grinds the beauty, the sweetness out of the human soul? If this wish came true, would it not be Christmas indeed — Christmas for all men, Christmas all the year?

Hear! To-day the bells and I call you to the Christmas of mankind. For it has begun, and we shall not falter nor turn back until every man and woman and child in this land and in every land has a chance to live happily and to develop his mind and do the best of which he is capable. Generation after generation has learned from its mothers' lips the story of the birth of Christ, and slowly the words have borne flowers — and the fruit is the Great Change. The Great Change is the new faith, the new effort to secure for every man his full share of the means, the comforts, the health, the knowledge, the virtue, which humanize life. As we lift up our voices, the bells and I, to sound the joy of Christmas, we call to you: Approach this new faith with open hearts. Let us follow it fearlessly, wherever it may lead us, even though it lead us far from old and cherished beliefs. Dear they are indeed and hard to part with; but this new faith is too appealing, too bound up with all that is deepest, most tender, most necessary in human experience to be put aside.

Hear, oh, hear the Christmas bells! How they answer one another from end to end of the country, peal upon peal, chime upon chime! From every spire and tower they utter the good tidings of great joy, the tidings of the Great Change, the cry that no humane heart can resist: "Brotherhood! Brotherhood! Brotherhood!"

Listen! Heed! For this is the harvest time of love. Souls are closer drawn to other souls. All that we have read and thought and hoped comes to fruition at this happy time. Our spirits are astir. We feel within us a strong desire to serve. A strange, subtle force, a new kindness, animates man and child. A new spirit is growing in us. No longer are we content to relieve pain, to sweeten sorrow, to give the crust of charity. We dare to give friendship, service, the equal loaf of bread, the love that knows no difference of station.

Hear, oh, hear the Christmas bells! Everywhere, everywhere they remind the world: Forget not the poor, nor let the hope of the needy fail.

The bells and I sing and are glad for Christmas, the day of all those who labour and keep the world alive. For them we sing and we shall not be still. The bells and I sing the workers of the world, on the Day of Him who was a boy in the carpenter's shop. This is the spirit of Christmas, that they whose lives are useful, whose deeds are good should receive the gift of gold, frankincense and myrrh. Should they stop their labour for a season, the world would starve. The stars would look down upon a world of silent cities, upon a devastated earth. Punctual as the bells the workers come and go. In winter's cold and summer's heat they hasten to the work of the world. Nothing halts them — sickness, fatigue, grief nor death. The mills of the world turn hourly, daily. We can tell the minute of their coming and going to their tasks; day after day, month after month, year after year the procession of the workers passes our doors. Through thousands of years have they been faithful, and Christmas shall open our hearts and let us say that in their lives the whole world lives.

Listen! Between the swelling peals of the Christmas bells, do you not hear the tramp of countless feet? Behold the workers have marched in the night toward the land of their hearts' desire. In the night of long ages they have heard the call of the Great Change and at length they have answered. Through darkness, through anguish and horror they have risen to the awful height of manhood. Century by century they have grown in power and intelligence. Forever and forever onward chime the bells! There has been no halting in the vast journey mankind has come. Nothing has been wasted, nothing has been lost. Every effort has counted. Every purpose, every pulse has fulfilled its task; incessantly men have moved onward to the dawn of the Great Change.

Can you not see the wonders which the Christmas bells herald? Do they not sing to you of world-systems evolving and dissolving, coming and going like leaves upon the trees, like the human generations? And again they shall evolve into the Great Change. As the notes of the bells rise, blend, and melt away, so have the life-songs of old civilizations swelled to the heavens, echo upon echo, and sunk into silence. Persia, Greece, and Rome have flourished and decayed. The civilization of Briton, Frenchman, German, American is passing, changing into the broader, nobler ideals of the Great Change — liberty, equality, and brotherhood.

Listen with your hearts. In a land but your will away from you, hear, oh, hear the Christmas bells ring, the winds blow, the rivers run, the earth break forth into flowers and the trees burst into leaf! Hear the birds singing and mating, and hear children freed from labour shouting in the streets, young men and maidens smiling and marrying, old people praising God that the Great Change has come in their day. "We have died to live again. We have suffered that we may rejoice and be glad. What matters it — all upheavals, all revolutions, all systems sent to wreck, if the Great Change comes afterward?"

Then ring all the bells on earth! 'Tis Christmas Day in the morning of brotherhood. Ring man's great joy from pole to pole, from sea to sea! Tug with mighty arms at the bell rope that the sound may ring out full and far and long! Light the world's Christmas tree with stars. Heap offerings upon its mighty branches. Bring the Yule-log to the world-fireplace. Deck the world-house with holly and mistletoe and proclaim everywhere the Christmas of the human race!

FINIS